CARTHAGE

CARTHAGE

GILBERT PICARD

Charles - Picard, Gilbert

Translated from the French by
MIRIAM and LIONEL KOCHAN

FREDERICK UNGAR PUBLISHING CO.
NEW YORK

CONTENTS

ILLUSTRATIONS

I

THE DISCOVERY OF A NEW WORLD

OUR civilisation was born over five thousand years ago in a domain which today is no longer completely our own: the large alluvial valleys of South-West Asia from Egypt to the Indus Valley. We are bound by a continuous tradition to the cities, kingdoms, and empires of the Pharaohs and Chaldeans, and even to the Mohenjo-daro culture —the furthest away and the most recently discovered. It is enough to recall that our system of writing, the essential instrument of all our thought, was invented by the Phoenicians about 2,500 years ago and this fundamental acquisition, which has not been essentially enriched since, represents the outcome of age-long endeavours made by the intellectual élite of the whole "fertile crescent".

The civilised world was completely identified with the Near East, today one of the most poverty-stricken areas of the world, for two and a half millennia—from the birth of the first kingdoms of Egypt and Sumer in about 3,500 B.C., until about 1,000 B.C. This is a period as long as that which separates us from the time when the first Europeans of our race, the Greeks, began to develop their own civilisation. But about the first millennium B.C., a historic phenomenon occurred, similar in many ways to the great movement which, after a further interval of 2,500 years, added a new continent to Europe's territory and which is still today taken as the point of departure for the last of the great periods into which our history is traditionally divided. It can legitimately be said that eastern navigators discovered a new world which was first, for six or seven centuries, a land for them to explore, exploit and colonise, before it took the place of older sources of civilisation, worn out and withered by over-long effort.

This was really the discovery of a foreign land, until then completely unknown. The Egyptians themselves, who lived at the west of the civilised world, had no conception of the lands situated beyond the Libyan desert. They readily undertook long journeys towards Syria across the desert, even though it was infested by pillaging Bedouins, or by sea from the port of Byblos; when opportunity offered, they fought the savage Nubians of the Upper Nile, or embarked on the Red Sea for the land of Punt. But for them the country to the West was the other world, steeped in mystery and visited only by the dead.

It is not surprising that the first sailors to venture into these unknown regions should expect to find them full of marvels and horrors. V. Bérard and his son J. Bérard claim that the Odyssey and the legend of the Argonauts preserve some of the tales brought back by these first explorers. This interpretation would appear more satisfactory than others which have since challenged it. Monsters and giants, sorcerers and magicians were undoubtedly invented by some boastful sailor—or by the poet who gathered his words. But the perils of difficult seas, unknown coasts, savage populations, at times anthropophagic, such as the Laestrygones of Ulysses, and almost always dangerous and barbarous, were not imaginary. If the explorer was not, like Ulysses, thrown involuntarily into this fearful world by the malignity of a divine enemy, then he must have been impelled by powerful motives. We have some inkling of these motives and will describe them shortly. But before anything else, boats capable of tackling the adventure, and crews to man them, were needed. Without the support of the Spanish and Portuguese monarchies in the fourteenth and fifteenth centuries A.D., neither Christopher Columbus nor Vasco da Gama could have put to sea. The discovery of the western basin of the Mediterranean was first made possible by the development of maritime powers in the Aegean Sea and on the Syrian coasts, closely linked by economic and cultural relations with the continental empires.

These had developed in the valleys of the great sub-tropical rivers, because of the exceptional fertility of the alluvium irrigated by the floods. This not only supplied food for the riverside dwellers, but also a sufficiently large surplus for them to indulge in those marginal activities which are at the basis of all civilisation. These essentially agricultural societies were inward-looking and needed some sort of antennae to make contact with the outside world. This rôle had been filled from time immemorial by the Phœnician city of Byblos, the outlet for Egypt and the point of contact between her and Mesopotamia. In the second millennium new maritime powers arose on all the coasts and on the islands of the Aegean Sea. The most brilliant of these was based on Crete; in the seventeenth century, the powerful Minos dynasty of Cnossos succeeded in founding a "thalassocracy" which controlled the whole of the eastern basin of the Mediterranean. Admirably situated at an equal distance from Syria, Egypt and the Balkan peninsula, the Cretans seem to have been the first men bold enough to cross the straits separating the two basins of the inland sea.

The Greeks of the Classical period still recounted how the second Minos, the grandson of the founder of the Empire, had met his death on an expedition to Sicily. Minoan prosperity was as brief as it was brilliant, but maritime hegemony passed immediately to the Achæans, the vanguard of the Hellenic peoples, who from the Peloponnese had conquered the southern coasts of Asia Minor and the island of Cyprus. The Achæans in turn succumbed before 1,000 B.C. to the assaults of another Hellenic tribe, the Dorians, and this invasion temporarily put an end to Greek control of the seas. The Phœnicians then profited from this to resume sole control of all navigation. Learning from the experience of their rivals, the Tyrians no longer limited themselves to local trade but in their turn organised distant expeditions westwards.

Other peoples, who are still only vaguely known and whom the classical Greeks designated by the more or less conventional names of Pelasgians, Carians or Leleges, were closely related to the Cretans by culture if not by race. Their rivalry with the Minoans or Phœnicians certainly gave rise to bloody conflict but it contributed equally powerfully to the extension of civilisation in the unknown lands of the West.

The maritime states were less vast and less populated than the great monarchies; sometimes they consisted only of a single city. Nor did they have at their disposal an agricultural production comparable to that of the monarchies. But they had been able to raise themselves to a quasi-equal footing because they brought to the monarchies the raw materials absent from the latter's economy. The wealth derived from agricultural prosperity had given birth to thousands of industries, but these now required metallic minerals which existed only in insufficient quantities in the alluvial plains and even in the belts of mountains. Cyprus owed its rapid development to its copper mines. Nevertheless, the metal was only usable as an alloy for tin, almost non-existent in the East. Ezekiel (XXVII, 12) tells us that silver, iron, tin and lead were supplied by a distant country, Tarshish, which can almost certainly be identified as southern Spain. It is at first surprising that supplies of essential materials should have depended on such a distant and precarious trade. But even when only stone was still in use, men had been willing to bring particular types of obsidian or silex from very far away. At first, western tin arrived by stages in the East, before direct relations were established between the two extreme shores of the Mediterranean. However, it was obviously preferable to avoid the long delays and expenses of such trade. Moreover, tin was not the only resource of the West: Spain, which did not produce it in sufficient quantity herself, took advantage of very ancient contacts established along the Atlantic coasts to obtain it from the mysterious islands of the Cassiterides. Thus Aegean sailors carried valuable freight, to be sold at a profit which would rapidly make them forget the perils they had faced to get it. Herodotus tells us that Colæos, the first Ionian arrival in Spain in the Eldorado of Tarshish ruled by the benign Arganthonios, made a fabulous fortune from that single expedition (630 B.C.).

Mention can also be made in this context of the wealth in gold, silver, ivory, monkeys and peacocks brought back by Solomon on the boats which his friend Hiram, King of Tyre, had obligingly permitted him to attach to the Phœnician fleet.

Such profits explain the rapid growth and luxury of the maritime civilisations. But this did not ensure them a stability comparable with that in the great agricultural monarchies. Their wealth aroused the envy of other sea-faring peoples, further intensified by the desire to eliminate favoured rivals; envy of the great monarchies themselves, tempted to assume direct control of these intermediaries who seemed to enjoy too large a share of good fortune; envy, above all, of the bar-barians, all the more dangerous as the maritime civilisations developed at the extremities of the civilised world and at the very gateway of the Aryan hordes who descended from the plains of Eastern Europe towards the warm seas, fascinated by the existence and easy life of the south. This Aryan thrust seems to have been the principal factor of instability in the second millennium between 1,400 and 1,200 B.C. The states founded by the vanguard, the Achæan and Hittite king-doms, were quickly permeated by eastern culture and collapsed beneath the attacks of their kin who had remained barbarians. The repercussion provoked a general upheaval amongst all the sea-faring nations. Ugarit, the point of contact between Cyprus and northern Phœnicia, was entirely destroyed in about 1,200 B.C. Sidon in turn succumbed to the attacks of the Philistines. However, the wave lost strength as it moved further from its point of origin, and Rameses III was able to drive the raiders back from the frontiers of Egypt. Greek epic tradition retained nothing of this great upheaval except the conflict between the Achæan confederation and the town of Ilium, enriched by control of the Hellespont. The date of the Trojan War and, more important, its exact place in the train of events that we suspect rather than know, are still under discussion. But Homer was not mistaken when he made the sequel to the Iliad the wanderings of Ulysses in the West. The men from the sea who attacked Egypt were not simple pirates, but uprooted people in search of a place to settle. Failing to find it in the East, like the Philistines who then settled in

Palestine, to which their name is still attached, some of the "outcasts" undoubtedly resigned themselves to seeking sanctuary in the virgin and barbarous lands of the West. It was formerly thought that the names of the Tyrrhenians, Etruscans and Sardinians could be read in the list of vanquished enemies, engraved in thanksgiving in Egyptian temples. These interpretations are today contested, but it remains probable that the founders of the Tuscan civilisation, which reveals incontestable affinities with the East, left their native land in the great upheaval which has just been outlined.

We have now reached approximately 1,000 B.C. The catastrophe which struck almost all the maritime powers of the ancient world, spared only Tyre. The Dorians, masters of Crete, scarcely bothered with naval enterprises and the Tyrians had only to use the routes opened up by the Aegeans without fear of competition. They advanced to the extreme limits of the western sea and at the end of it discovered the fabulous realm of Tarshish, the ancient Eldorado, which added to the products of the fertile Andalusia all the mineral wealth brought from Spain as well as that which came down the ocean coasts from the frozen countries of the North. The hospitable kings who governed it granted the Phœnicians a concession; Gades, the future Cadiz, where Melqart the "King of Tyre" compared by the Greeks to Hercules, was worshipped, according to Asiatic rites, until the time of the Roman Empire. On the African coast an equivalent position was occupied at Lixus, and Melqart was entitled to assert his control over the whole strait dominated by his "columns". For eight centuries no boat could cross or even approach it without a safe-conduct from the servants of the "god".

This annexation of Tarshish had the same importance for Tyre as the possession of India for England in the eighteenth and nineteenth centuries. A whole network of control posts, fortresses and ports was established to ensure access to it. But ancient navigation consisted only of coastwise trade; every night, unless it was absolutely impossible, the boat was hauled on to dry land on a safe beach. The existence of regular traffic with Tarshish therefore required control over the Maghreb coast, unless a détour was made by way of Italy and Provence or a direct crossing made by Sicily or Sardinia to the Balearics: hazardous navigation in the Gulf of Lions was enough to invalidate these solutions even if their length had not in itself made them barely feasible. The Phœnicians ensured control of the middle route by controlling eastern Sicily, Sardinia and the Balearics. But the African route would always remain the best and the most jealously guarded.

The facts just cited explain how we accept the very early dates handed down by tradition for the foundation of Gades, Lixus and Utica (end of the twelfth century B.C.). This is despite the scepticism of many modern scholars and in the absence of archæological discoveries confirming the texts. It is logical that Tyre should have discovered Tarshish at the time when she enjoyed a greater degree of freedom of the seas, during the eclipse of the Aegean-Hellenics brought about by the Dorian invasion, and before she had to face the Assyrian menace at home and the resumption of Greek activity at sea.

It can also be seen that the occupation of Africa was never an end in itself for Tyre. The country was in fact far from offering as many attractions as Andalusia, or even the coasts of Italy or Gaul. From the mouth of the Medjerda to the Columns of Hercules, the Tellian Atlas forms an almost unbroken barrier of inhospitable mountains bristling with thick forests, inaccessible because of wild animals. The eastern shore of Tunis, separated from the steppes by the hills of the Sahel and covered before cultivation by a jungle of wild olive and mastic-trees, seemed less hostile, but it was guarded by swamps, and good anchorage was very rare. It must be noted in passing that the Ancients were always mistaken regarding the general orientation of this coast, undoubtedly because they avoided the base of the Gulf of Gabès (Little Syrtis) as far as possible; they looked on it more as a lake, the Triton, antechamber of the "great Chotts", than as a marine bay. They therefore aligned the Sahel with the prolongation of Tell and almost failed to recognise the difference in latitude between Tripolitania and Tunisia. Did this error, for which the Tyrian navigators, the first to explore the coast, were certainly responsible, prevent them recognising that the country they were going to make into a new Phœnicia turned to the east, offering the open doorway of the Maghreb? In any case, they understood the importance of the promontory formed by the last secondary ranges of the Atlas, a real hinge of the two Mediterranean basins: the widest bay of the whole African coast stretches between Cape Bon and the escarpments of Porto Farina. Tradition recounts that the Tyrians took possession of it from the end of the twelfth century B.C., *i.e.* at the same time as their relations with Tarshish took the form of regular trade. In fact, according to Pliny, the foundation of the Temple of Apollo at Utica goes back to that date; eleven centuries later, its beams of cedar cut in Lebanon by the first colonists were still pointed out by the priests for admiration.

Utica is situated on the north bank of the gulf, near the mouths of the Medjerda. This river, known to the Ancients as the Bagradas is, although the largest in Tunisia, only a "wadi" better fed than the

[1] Tomb discovered at Utica by P. Cintas. This monument has been transformed several times and has been used at various burials over a very long period. It would seem that it was first used before the seventh century B.C. The architecture is related to ancient Phoenician and Cypriot tombs.

[2] Two black limestone terminal figures at Carthage, at the thermae of Antoninus. They date from the middle of the second century A.D. and undoubtedly represent prisoners captured by the Romans in the north of the Oran Sahara. The one on the left is certainly the most beautiful portrait of a Libyan bequeathed by antiquity. The shaven skull is decorated by a plait at the crown—still worn by certain Berbers. This *choucha* retains the *baraka*. Its sacred value is increased here by the crescent-shaped amulet, the emblem of Tanit-Caelestis. The negro on the right represents the Ethiopian tribes who lived, mingled with the Libyans, throughout the Sahara.

[3] The fountain of a thousand amphorae, the only spring in Carthage. It flows into the sea under the hill of Borj-Jedid. First channelled by the Carthaginians; the arches date from the Roman period.

[4] Stele of the priest with a child, found by stone hunters in 1921. It led to the discovery of the tophet. The bas-relief, which dates from the end of the fifth century B.C. or the beginning of the fourth, is the strongest pictorial evidence of the reality of child-sacrifice. The personage is a *Kohen*, a priest, clad, like those of Egypt, in a transparent linen robe. For attitude and head-dress compare the stele of Ba'alyton which originates from Oum el Amad in Phoenicia and is almost contemporary (G. Contenau, *Man. d'arch. orient.*, III, p.1476, fig. 897): an example of the eastern style to be compared with that of Ill. 17. The priest raises his head towards the god in supplication and to offer him the child he carries.

[5] View of part of the tophet. The level corresponds to the last period of the cippus (end of the 6th and beginning of 5th century). The monuments in position have been protected by the construction of a Roman arch. In the foreground are the pots which contain the ashes of the victims.

[6] Three vases from the chapel, the oldest Phoenician objects discovered in Africa: amphora with twisted handles, which was buried under a wall, as a foundation deposit, water sprinkler and dove-shaped vase. The decoration is related to the Cycladic geometric style. Date: middle of the eighth century B.C.

[7] Greek black-figured vase (Corinthian).

[8] Stele from the tophet representing a funeral offering: a woman, kneeling by a hillock covering a tomb, is about to pour the libation contained in the wine jug she holds in her hand. This is evidence of a cult of the dead at the tophet, which was undoubtedly addressed to Dido. Date: third century B.C. The costume and the style show Greek influence.

[9] Attic dish, found with the Greek vase, in tombs at Carthage. They are both evidence of the active Greco-Punic trade before the sixth century.

[10] Sixth century Greek statuette, discovered at Carthage. It represents a goddess clad in an embroidered gown. This garment was later imitated by the Carthaginians (see Ill. 71). She holds a circular object, probably a dulcimer.

others. Its delta, constantly enlarged by new alluvia, is so different now from what it was three thousand years ago that it would be ill-advised and vain to try to reconstitute the countryside where the Tyrians settled. Moreover, methodical excavations have only been carried on since 1947. It is not surprising, therefore, that the only pre-Roman monuments discovered were tombs, or that the oldest of these only went back to the seventh or perhaps the eighth century B.C. The antiquity of the foundation could only be seriously doubted if, as at Carthage, a sanctuary founded by the first colonists were discovered, where the oldest inscriptions would date the installation. But if such a "tophet" exists at Utica, it remains hidden under several feet of alluvial deposit. We do not even know where the port was situated; as for the Temple of Apollo and its thousand-year-old beams, they have shared the fate of many a famous ancient sanctuary, whose fame was so great an attraction to pillagers that not one stone was left standing.

This lack—possibly temporary—of all ancient Phœnician objects is not peculiar to Utica. Nowhere in Africa, neither on the site of a Punic town nor in native dwellings, has any important object so far been discovered that can be dated earlier than 750 B.C. It is tempting, when faced with this established fact to ask, as several scholars have done, whether the Ancients might not have made the first settlements by foreign sailors on African soil appear older than they were. However, we do not think it necessary to share such scepticism. In fact, it is enough to recall the conditions in which the first Phœnician trading stations were set up, and the state of the population then occupying Africa to understand that their presence left only insignificant traces, easily effaced by time.

A settlement such as Utica was, as we have seen, only created as a factor function of the trade with Tarshish. The Book of Kings relates that the western fleet only returned to Lebanese ports three years after leaving them. This slowness is explained by the circumstances of ancient navigation. The crossing was interrupted at the autumn equinox, when the boats were drawn on to dry land and reconditioned; the sailor could, when necessary, transform himself into a cultivator because he did not take to the sea again until the spring equinox. Even during the six months available for navigation, each day's journey never exceeded some twenty-five miles including the time spent at every port, so that two summers does not seem an over-long delay for travelling along the southern coast of the Mediterranean, some two thousand five hundred miles. There had therefore to be a safe port of call somewhere around the middle of the journey, large

enough and comfortable enough for the crews to winter there. This
was the rôle of Utica, whose very nature precluded it from having a
fixed population of any great size. Food resources, which could only
be small in a place lacking all hinterland, were inevitably reserved for
the ships' crews. Workmen necessary to the repair of the ships,
soldiers indispensable for defence, some merchants, and administra-
tive, military and religious people were the only personnel living in
the town. We may suppose that these exiles, mostly separated from
their families, all hoped to return to their homeland and that, if by
mischance, they died before this happened, their bodies were taken
back to Phœnicia as soon as possible. There is therefore scarcely any
prospect of finding important archaic necropolises. As the archæologist generally establishes the chronology of a town by excavating its
tombs, it would be imprudent here, deprived of this basis, to challenge
the information provided by the ancient authors, especially where
their archives contain carefully recorded dates of the foundation of
towns or temples.

These Phœnician trading stations, quite similar, as P. Cintas has
rightly noted, to those which the first European sailors established on
African and Asian coasts, would have developed differently if they
had been, not simply relay-posts along the route to Tarshish, but
centres of active commerce with the natives. For this, however, the
country would have had to supply commodities appreciated in the
East, and for the natives to be willing to accept Phœnician merchandise in exchange. Amongst the treasures of Tarshish enumerated in
the Book of Kings, ivory and monkeys could have originated in
Africa, but they were probably delivered to the Phœnicians by the
Tartessians, who procured them in Morocco. The Africans with whom
the people of Utica came into contact were only wretched savages,
extremely wild and very poor. But these barbarians are of interest in
that they were more fortunate than the Phœnicians themselves in
perpetuating their race, language and some of their customs up to the
present day.

In the very distant past—ten thousand years possibly before our
era, when men were still only using tools made from splintered stone
—Homo Sapiens conquered Northern Africa, occupied until then by
pygmies of the Neanderthal type. The white race of Mechta el Arbi
to which these conquerors belonged had characteristics close to those
of Cro-Magnon Europeans. Prehistorians call the "civilisation" they
established on the Barbary coasts "Ibero-Maurusian". It may have
lasted until the arrival of the Carthaginians. Theirs was a wretched
mode of life, little conducive to progress. Later, other men of Mediter-

ranean race occupied the Pre-Saharian steppes surrounding salt-water lagoons. They are known as Capsians. Capsian remains are often called "snaileries". They are actually fossilised kitchen hearths, their ashes full of shells of gasteropods, the most important food, and also stone tools.

Towards the end of their long existence, some five thousand years before our era, the Capsians learned new techniques, undoubtedly taught by foreigners, mainly negroid, who infiltrated among them; these included the polishing of stone and, above all, the domestication of animals. Stock farming was to become the essential resource of African man. Neolithic tools are exactly similar to those used by the population of the Nile valley at the same period.

No insuperable gap existed up till that time between the Maghreb and the Sudan. The Sahara, criss-crossed by rivers, was covered with grassy steppe. But the rise in temperature which freed Europe from ice, withered and sterilised the sub-tropical zone. The vegetation and animals, isolated by this change in the north of the desert, were thenceforth condemned to slow extinction. However, elephants, ostriches, lions, snakes and crocodiles succeeded in resisting it for quite a long time. New invaders mixed with the Capsians or drove them back and destroyed the Ibero-Maurusians. They only continued to exist in the Canaries, where their descendants formed the strange Guanches population, discovered and soon destroyed by the Europeans in the fourteenth century A.D.

The men who then settled in North Africa were called Libyans by the Greeks. The people now known as Berbers—a simple corruption of the Latin Barbarus—are certainly their direct descendants, Arabised to a greater or lesser degree depending on their location. The Saharan Tuareg represent the purest element, that is, the race which has best preserved its ancestral tradition. From the dawn of history, the Libyans occupied the domain over which the surviving groups of Berbers are scattered today, that is to say the whole of the Maghreb and the Sahara from Egypt to the Atlantic; to the south of the Atlas mountains they co-habited with a number of negro tribes.

The Libyan group, more than anything else, is a linguistic unit. Undoubtedly the dialects spoken by the various ancient tribes differed—less however than the modern Berber tongues, which have been profoundly transformed by Arab influence. Moreover, Libyan is very poorly known. Apart from the names of men and places, the only texts which have reached us are inscriptions engraved on stone, especially in eastern Tunisia and the Constantine area, which date for the most part from the last two centuries before the Christian era.

They are couched in an alphabet with simple geometric forms, written from bottom to top. This the Tuaregs still use, with very minor alterations, under the name of Tifinagh. The value of the letters is certain but their interpretation has aroused violent discussion. Moreover, linguists have not yet succeeded in reconstituting "common Libyan" from which the ancient and modern dialects derive. It is like trying to study the Indo-European languages from a few Greek inscriptions and the dialect of the French and German provinces. Meanwhile, it is generally admitted that Libyan is related to ancient Egyptian and with it forms the Hamitic family.

Even less is known of the race than of the language. The only certainty is that the Berbers are white; blonde elements can even be found among them, probably of distant Nordic origin. As far back as its arrival in North Africa, the ethnic group was undoubtedly composed of a mixture of varied human elements from the Mediterranean; since then it has been strongly crossed with negro blood.

The Libyan Berbers thus did not differ fundamentally from other human groups living along the shores of the Mediterranean. The strength of the race, its extraordinary resistance, which excited the admiration of the ancient peoples, still continues today. Some individuals have shown the highest intellectual qualities, but, in general, the group is characterised by its adherence to a barbarous mode of life. This is all the more extraordinary as it has on several occasions been incorporated in the most advanced civilisations, in which some of its members have actively participated. No historian has yet provided a satisfactory explanation of this phenomenon. It has been suggested that the various foreign rulers which succeeded each other in the country prevented the development of a local civilisation. But scarcely a people in the world has not at some time in its history been dominated by a more developed nation and has not profited from what the conquerors brought, even after having freed itself from the yoke. The Libyan Berbers enthusiastically adopted Punic, Roman and Islamic culture in turn. But a section always remained barbarian and that section most frequently succeeded in submerging the more developed elements; or it encircled them, as though they were alien bodies in a resisting organism.

The explanation must rather be sought in the exceptionally hard natural conditions which the natives never succeeded in mastering, and which also defeated the foreign civilisations, so that localities where the most primitive way of life was perpetuated were left side by side with the more developed regions. This powerlessness of man in the face of unproductive and hostile nature has been evident since the dawn of history. It is significant that the first Libyans could not utilise the conquered land any better than the Neolithic populations they drove out or annihilated. Stockbreeding and hunting remained their main means of subsistence. Industry, which was left almost entirely to women, only produced crudely shaped pottery and a few wooden and leather objects. Scarcely any metal instruments are known, other than those brought by foreign merchants. Clothing and dwellings were almost non-existent. The tribes roamed about unceasingly, following their flocks or in quest of game. Those living in the south who came into contact with the negro cultivators, fleeced them unmercifully. This parasitism, which has assured the survival of the Tuareg today, undoubtedly explains the apparently paradoxical fact that some of the Saharans, such as the Garamantes of Fezzan, whose power was already pointed out by Herodotus, were often wealthier than their kinsmen of the Maghreb. Intellectual life stagnated at the lowest level. Thus, religious beliefs, similar to those of the American Indians or the more backward inhabitants of Oceania, consisted only of a vague awareness of an indeterminate supernatural force, of which physical phenomena, such as the exceptional powers of certain vegetables and animals, the abilities of privileged human beings, and the state of exaltation aroused by social manifestations appear to have been the various factors. Sorcerers manipulated this sacred power with the aid of fairly simple processes and directed it as they wished in a favourable or harmful manner.

The dead played an important part in religious belief and were the object of a sort of cult. Their tombs are the only monuments. Some of these, built of large slabs of stone, exactly resemble European megaliths, the work of an Atlantic civilisation in the Bronze Age. The Libyans were still constructing dolmens under the Roman Empire, over a thousand years after they had ceased to be built in Europe. Can an ethnic relationship between them and the pre-Aryans of Europe be deduced from this? The historian cannot definitely say— no more than he can determine the existence and nature of the contacts which might have existed between the Proto-Libyans and other mysterious river-dwellers of the Western Mediterranean: Iberians, Sardinians and Siculi.

It should be easier to measure the influence of Eastern civilisations. One of these, Egypt, was in immediate contact with the Libyans of the East; the identification of Neolithic objects in the Nile valley and north-west Africa seems to indicate the existence of commercial interchange. But these relationships disappeared in historical times. The Egyptians were well acquainted with the Libyans in their own country, as invaders, tributaries or vassals, and used them as mercenaries. They preserved peaceful and even cultural relations with some of the tribes, particularly those which inhabited the oasis of Ammon, today Sioua. It was previously believed that the cult of Ammon extended very widely towards the West; rupestral engravings in Southern Algeria, representing a ram with a very complicated headdress, had been interpreted as images of the god. This hypothesis has been abandoned today. On the other hand, recent excavations have found no trace of Pharaonic occupation in Cyrenaica; and not one Egyptian object has ever been discovered in North Africa that had not been brought back by the Punics or the Romans.

Scholars studying the rupestral engravings in the Sahara have observed ornamental motifs, such as the spiral, which are characteristic of Aegean art. It is even more interesting to note the resemblance between the representations of chariots, which often appear on petroglyphs attributed to the Garamantes of Fezzan, and those of the Mycenæan painters; in both places a galloping horse is represented in the same style, which makes it seem to fly over the earth. These chariots were very important to the Garamantes. The camel was not yet used in Africa—it did not appear there until the fourth century B.C.—and the distribution of rupestral engravings proves that travellers crossed the Sahara, which was undoubtedly less dry than it is today, on horses harnessed to light vehicles. The sources of some ancient Greek legends, for example that of Perseus and the Gorgon, are located in the region of the Syrtes, and the island of the Lotoseaters where Ulysses almost forgot Ithaca, is now identified as Djerba. Again, in the seventh century, it was Cretan fishermen who guided the colonists from Thera (now Santorin) and their chief Battos to Cyrenaica, on the advice of the Delphic oracle. It is therefore possible that the Cretans disembarked on the coasts of Africa at the time when Minos was in full glory. But no object has yet been found to bear indisputable witness to their passage.

Thus everything combines to show that the Proto-Libyans found themselves cut off, by their own poverty, from the evolution which gave birth to civilisation on the other shores of the Mediterranean. This isolation would have continued even longer if the Phœnicians, for economic and political reasons completely foreign to Africa, had not imposed a completely new colonial policy on Tyre towards the end of the ninth century.

II

THE BIRTH OF CARTHAGE

ALL the ancient authors agree that in 814 B.C. part of the population of Tyre, guided by Elissa or Dido, a princess of the royal family, left Phœnicia without thought of return, and founded a town near Utica which they called "Qart Hadasht". We have made this into "Carthage". Then again, archæologists, working on the site of this city, have found a certain number of objects imported from the east which may be dated from the eighth century B.C. and bear witness to the settlement of a fairly numerous population.

This mass emigration was till then unprecedented in Phœnicia. Other eastern peoples had undoubtedly left *en masse* for the West in the last centuries of the second millennium. At the very time when Dido left Tyre, a few Greek cities, particularly Ionia and Euboea, began to resume the Aegean tradition by sending colonists to the coasts of southern Italy and the shores of the Black Sea. But the Phœnicians were reluctant to leave their own country, finally and *en masse*, for a distant land. Their only conquest of any extent was the eastern part of Cyprus, in the neighbourhood of their own Lebanon.

But Dido and her companions seem right from the start to have wanted, if not completely to break all links with their native land, at least to create a settlement in Africa which could be self-sufficient. Even the name they gave to their city bears witness to this. M. Forrer recently drew attention to the meaning of Qart Hadasht, which means not only "new town" but "new capital". They intended to create a new Tyre which would be able to dispense with the old capital.

Tradition explains this rupture by internal conflict, a rivalry between two branches of the reigning family. In fact, it seems more likely that it was an external danger which imposed a bold, almost desperate solution. Between about 1,200 and 900 B.C. the decadence of the "great empires" (Egyptian, Hittite, Mitanni) which fought with each other for power in Syria, permitted the free development of autochthonous states of medium size in that area, amongst which a certain equilibrium was established. It was at this time that the Hebrews created their kingdom, which split up after the glorious reigns of David and Solomon. The Benhadad dynasty made Damascus a prosperous capital. Further north, the last Hittites, increasingly mixed with Semitic Aramaeans, governed Carchemish and Aleppo. This fragmentation of their ancient country into principalities of almost equal force could only be favourable to the autonomy of the Phœnician cities, which were ready to deal with them on an equal footing.

But after 1,000 B.C. a new imperialist power began to expand its domination to the west of the Euphrates, a domination founded on a policy so brutal that men sighed for the former conquerors. This was Assyria, which under Ashornazirpal (884-860) for the first time thrust its devastating armies as far as the Mediterranean. Tyrians and Sidonians soon recognised that neither their ships nor their walls could shield them from invaders who were as skilful in the art of siege as in the strategy of open warfare. From 876, they had to resign themselves to paying a tribute, and the insatiable greed of their new masters quickly rendered the burden of payment intolerable. Obviously the best means of escaping this was to create an autonomous centre where the wealth of the West could grow, far enough away to make exactions impossible.

Other causes, originating in the west itself are less clearly seen. It is certain that from the beginning of the first millennium, Gaul and Spain were disturbed by the great movements of mankind. The one least difficult to reconstruct thrust the Celts from Central Europe towards the west, until in the sixth century they dominated the major part of Gaul and north Spain. Tartessos was undoubtedly not directly affected but its commercial connections on the Atlantic coasts might have come to some harm. It was tempting for the Phœnicians to profit from these events by substituting themselves for the intermediaries whom they could not be certain of keeping indefinitely under their control. In fact, after the eighth century, their rivals, who were strongly entrenched in Italy, did seek to divert part of the trade with the East to their own account: Greeks, who multiplied their colonies on the southern coasts of the Peninsula and Sicily; Etruscans, who in their turn built merchant ships and privateers. The Phœnicians were thus in danger of losing control of the straits which joined the two Mediterranean basins. In fact, their rivals soon appeared at Tartessos where they received a warm welcome. Diodorus also describes the rivalry between Etruscans and Carthaginians for possession of the "Fortunate Islands" in the Atlantic Ocean, which are undoubtedly Madeira. The monopoly of supplying the east with indispensable metals was obviously too easy a source of wealth for the Tyrians, who had only captured it because of the collapse of the other maritime powers, to be able to retain it without a struggle after their restoration. This is an absolutely analogous historical process to the great battles of the mercantile powers in the 17th and 18th centuries A.D., following the period of the discoveries and the establishment of the Spanish and Portuguese Empires. But Tyre was situated too far from the scene of battle to wage war efficiently. It became necessary to transfer to the west the political and economic direction of Phœnician interests.

The leaders of Tyrian policy might have thought it sufficient to reinforce and transform Utica. If they did not do so, it is undoubtedly because the site of the old trading station did not seem adequate to meet the needs of a large population. The peninsula of Carthage, on the other side of the Medjerda, was the perfect answer to the need for security *vis-à-vis* the continent, with which the Phœnician founders were particularly concerned. It consisted of a group of sandstone hills, joined to the mainland on the western and southern sides by two sandy isthmuses, the former wide and negotiable to traffic, the latter— which the Romans called *Taenia*—very narrow and cut by a gully. These two strands cut off a vast lagoon to the south-west, shallow and often evil-smelling, but it abounded in fish and offered a natural harbour to vessels of small draught: this was the Gulf of Tunis. To the north of the peninsula lay the Gulf of Utica, which has today been reduced to a lagoon by the formation of a third off-shore bar. The hills form an arc, opening towards the west. The northern branch overlooks the sea from high inhospitable cliffs. The southern is separated from the waters of the bay, bounded on the east by a coastal plain bordered by sandy coves. Here the first colonists settled, possibly using a lagoon near the base of the *taenia* as a harbour. The oldest sanctuary showing material evidence of their presence has been found here, on a beach. To ensure their immediate safety, they needed only to occupy the nearest hill. It has been claimed that Dido obtained this hill from the natives by a ruse worthy of a Levantine merchant. She paid the price of a plot large enough to be covered by one ox-hide and then cut this up into strips so that it encircled the whole base of the hill. Actually, this old wives' tale rests on a play of words: *byrsa*, the Punic name for this acropolis, means in Greek "the hide of an ox". It is much more probable that the Tyrians assured immediate control of the whole peninsula by barring the isthmus at its narrowest point, from the lake to the gulf. The advance defences of the town were later built there. The colonists reserved twenty or so square miles of cultivable land for themselves in addition to the narrow space necessary for their buildings—for which no more than some eight or ten acres were needed. Thus, the new town, like Babylon, was a sort of fortified area capable of being self-sufficient for at least some time, in case of blockade, and free from too close a dependence on the natives. These advantages, to which must be added a healthy and agreeable climate even during the hottest summers (the sirocco crosses the Gulf of Tunis and becomes cooler before it reaches Carthage) offset the few inconveniences such as the insufficient supply of drinking water—only one source of supply exists, known today as the "fountain of a thousand amphorae"—and the mediocrity of the natural ports, which had to be adapted by large-scale building.

The proud choice of the name "Qart Hadasht" shows that from the very beginning Dido and her companions were conscious of transferring the centre of Tyrian power to the West. Meanwhile, archæology and history agree in admitting the slow development of Carthage. Only towards the beginning of the seventh century, after more than a hundred years, did it emerge as a rich and powerful town. There is nothing extraordinary in this, when it is realised that the real causes of its creation continued to exist. Assyria, more powerful than ever under the Sargonids, gave the Phœnicians no respite. In 672 B.C. Asarhaddon punished Tyre, which had sought the protection of Egypt. Greek rivalry only became really dangerous in the West after 750 B.C., the date of the foundation of Syracuse. Then it increased for a century and a half as the pressure of emigrants grew, driven from Asia Minor first by Lydian domination—Crœsus reigned from 563 to 548 B.C.—and then by the Persian conquest. A continuous stream must therefore have brought new men and new wealth towards the town of Dido which was only really solidly established when it had assimilated this influx. Certain modern scholars who believe that the date of foundation can be brought up to the beginning of the seventh century should remember that the history of colonisation offers frequent examples of time-lag between the foundation of a new city and the moment when it really begins to live. Will future archæologists find many traces of New Amsterdam when they excavate New York and will they not be tempted to date its foundation from the eighteenth century or even later?

Historians today seem much more prudent than their predecessors, who were all too ready to think that facts handed down by tradition in the periods before the first historical works were worthless. Archæology has frequently confirmed, more or less directly, some of this legendary material. Italian excavators on the Palatine have recently found the foundations of huts which can be exactly dated at the middle of the eighth century, and were therefore contemporary with Romulus. Undoubtedly this historical element in tradition is, more often than not, reduced to dates or names, clothed in a myth. But this myth itself is not simply imaginative fiction. Born, usually, in a holy place, it bears the onus of explaining the forms of worship, the names of the gods or heroes, the strange appearance of certain monuments or the ceremonial rites. The myth offers a valuable record of institutions and the way of thought of the men who conceived it and spread it.

Thus the romantic story of the death of Dido throws light on the religious nature of Punic royalty and gives an idea of the birth of one of the city's principal cults.

The misfortunes of Elissa did not end in Africa. The Libyan king who permitted the exiles to settle in his land lost no time in falling in love with the unfortunate princess. She had always remained attached to the memory of her husband, more because of the survival of her love than from a sense of duty. Certain of meeting refusal if he declared himself openly, the king confided his passion to the principal citizens of the new town. They feared the consequences if he were disappointed—and with reason—and therefore adopted a somewhat disloyal ruse. They told the Queen that the Libyan had asked the Phœnicians to send instructors to teach his subjects the rules of civilised life. But who, they added, perfidiously, would consent to share the life of those barbarians? Dido reproached them for their scanty courage and devotion. They then revealed the king's real intention. The Queen asked only that she be permitted by a solemn ceremony to break the sacred ties binding her to her husband. She had a funeral pyre erected not far from her house, sacrificed numerous victims and, suddenly, threw herself into the flames. Her subjects, in despair and possibly repentant, took to worshipping her as a goddess, and this cult, which was celebrated at the actual place of her self-sacrifice, lasted until the destruction of Carthage. Such is the moving story told by Justin, Roman historian of the second century A.D. Its essentials were already contained in a passage by Timæus of Taormina, who lived five centuries earlier. The poets altered it according to the flights of their imagination. Virgil did not hesitate to age Dido by three or four centuries so that she might meet Aeneas and also had no scruples in explaining her suicide by the flight of the Trojans. At first sight, it is tempting to see in all this only a tale in the style of Mlle. de Scudéry; and all the psychological part of the story is certainly the work of the Greeks, who were both rationalist and sentimental in the style formed by the Museum of Alexandria during the Hellenistic period. But these scholars worked on material that one

of them had found in Carthage. By scratching slightly below the surface of the fable, an authentic Phœnician myth can be rediscovered
which ethnographers easily explain by comparison with other legends,
and particularly through descriptions of ritual practices whose
existence and meaning are beyond all doubt.

A number of primitive peoples believe that the prosperity of the
community and even of nature depends on a potential of sacred
energy, incarnate in the person of the chief of the tribe. This energy
diminishes with time. The only means of renewing it is to sacrifice
the king, who then becomes the object of worship. This death often
follows a religious marriage when the monarch unites himself to a
divinity representing Mother Earth, thus giving fertility to the earth,
animals and even men.

The legend of the death of Dido corresponds exactly to this ritual
theme. The "King of the Libyans" whom Dido was to marry represents the principal powers of the African earth that had to be recon-
ciled to the new colonists. The suicide of the Queen on her funeral
pyre is obviously a sacrifice. Moreover, the Phœnicians are known to
have practised royal sacrifice, traces of which have also been found
in Egypt and Crete. The Carthaginians, who were particularly superstitious and conservative, remained attached to this barbarous
practice until a very late date. In 480 B.C. the king, Hamilcar, killed
himself in the same way as Dido by throwing himself on to a sacrificial
pyre after being conquered by the Greeks at Himera, in Sicily. Again,
King Juba I of the Numidians, successors to the Carthaginian
civilisation, tried to burn himself and his city when he was conquered
by Cæsar in 46 B.C. But more often a less important victim was
substituted for the king, although close enough not to give the gods
cause to complain of the exchange; usually it was one of the king's
own sons. This explains the sacrifices of children, for which Carthage
is notorious.

These sacrifices were known from numerous texts—the most
detailed is a passage from Diodorus Siculus, transposed by Flaubert
in *Salammbô*. But material remains were not discovered until 1920.
Thousands of earthen vases were stacked twenty to thirty feet below
the surface near the old commercial port, in the district today called
Salammbo. They all contain the ashes of burned babies. Mixed with
them were stone monuments of quite varied form: sandstone cippae
or pointed limestone steles in the shape of obelisks. This melancholy
sanctuary is known as a *tophet*, from the Biblical name of that part of
the Valley of Ben Hinnom on the outskirts of Jerusalem, where the
Israelites also sacrificed children before this practice was brought

to an end in the seventh century B.C. by the pious King Josiah.

Child sacrifice was in fact a practice common to all the inhabitants of Canaan, that is to say, to the ancestors of the Hebrews as well as to those of the Phœnicians. The whole world knows the monstrous "Moloch" and can, like Flaubert, conjure up a vision of a bronze monster consuming the quivering victims within its white-hot body. The word, which is really *molk*, is found in inscriptions at Carthage and other African cities. But it is now known through the research of a German scholar, O. Eissfeldt, that it referred to the sacrifice and not to the god who demanded it.

The ancient peoples were as horrified as ourselves by these sacred murders and the barbarity of their perpetrators; Flaubert gives a description of this religious madness, inspired by the gatherings of the Aissaoua which he witnessed and which is undoubtedly psychologically if not historically exact. He used it to lead his awestruck reader into an inhuman world, freed from all the rules which regulate our morals and our aesthetic sense.

But this romantic interpretation of Carthage, as will be seen, is very far from reality. How could a civilised city, which knew and admired Hellenistic humanism, preserve until its destruction and even bequeath to its successors practices which have no equivalent except amongst the most savage Papuans?[1] In their inability to answer this question, some people have wished to thrust aside the evidence, deny the existence of child sacrifice, and see it as Greco-Latin "war propaganda". But the Romans, who said so much about the tortures of Regulus, never mentioned the *molk* in their anti-Punic diatribes, probably because, although the custom had not disappeared at the time of the Punic wars, it had not the same strong impact as in earlier centuries.

The explanation of this mystery would seem to be given by a recent archæological discovery which enables the practice of the *molk* to be linked to the legend of Dido. At the lowest level of the *tophet* Cintas discovered the ruins of a sort of chapel with a surface all in all not larger than six feet by nine. Rough labyrinthine walls of stone and earth surrounded a low room covered with a plaster dome, a minute courtyard and a small altar. A hole hollowed in the rock in the centre of the room held a few terra cotta vessels: one in the shape of a dove, with its beak forming a spout; a sort of gourd with an elongated neck; a saucer lamp moulded into a spout; and two tiny bowls. One of the walls concealed a foundation deposit: an amphora with

---

[1] Father A. Dupeyrat describes in *Vingt et un Ans chez les Papous* a sacrifice of a new-born child which he rightly compares to the Carthaginian *molk*.

coiled handles, painted in red on a light base. This modest treasure, today exhibited at the Bardo Museum, possibly belonged to one of Dido's companions, or at least to one of their sons. In any case, it is the oldest historical relic to be discovered in North Africa. Specialists in Greek ceramics recognise in the geometric decoration on the vases a style fashionable in the Aegean islands in about 750 B.C.

What is the significance of the monument itself? It resembles a tomb—but that would make it a cenotaph—and particularly, strangely enough, the *marabouts*, which present-day Berbers erect on the tombs of holy people who possessed the *baraka*, despite the disapproval of orthodox Islam thinkers. This connection might appear remote had not exactly similar constructions been found at Ugarit in Phœnicia, belonging to a royal necropolis and undoubtedly dedicated to the worship of deceased princes. The "chapel" of Carthage was probably built in memory of a king or an important personality. Its date scarcely permits any doubt but that this hero was Dido herself. Furthermore, Justin writes that the site of the Queen's funeral pyre, which became the centre of her cult, was erected at the extreme edge of the town. The *tophet* is situated exactly at the southern extremity of Carthage. A tumulus or some simple monument must have marked the place where the Queen was sacrificed. As a result of this, the relationship established between the initial self-immolation of Dido and child sacrifice can be understood. Diodorus tells us that the children were not chosen by chance. They were the sons of noble families, and when little slaves were fraudulently substituted, the gods showed their anger by delivering Carthage to its enemies. At first, it must have been the children of the king who were sacrificed instead of the king himself. Later, when Carthage became a republic, this fearful obligation extended to all the aristocracy. That is why the Punics hardly ever dared to substitute by magical process animals for human victims, as so many other peoples did and as even the rules of their religion would have, if need be, allowed them. They would have been risking the destruction of their city. Even when the city was destroyed, the Romans, who prohibited the sacrifice of innocent people, had to find a way to satisfy the terrible masters of Africa by offering them the blood of condemned men, thrown to the beasts in the amphitheatre. Without this, Ba'al and Tanit would have unleashed the most terrible misfortunes on the blasphemers who cheated them of their tribute of human blood.

The ancient peoples often accused the Carthaginians of having a sombre and savage nature, which exasperated the optimistic Greeks. The primary cause of this grim disposition, which contributed greatly to their downfall by making them hateful to their neighbours, was perhaps the oppression of a form of original sin, the sentiment which made them shed innocent blood in order to found a city, and caused the cruel gods unceasingly to demand yet more blood to permit the city to survive. It is remarkable that nations such as the Etruscans or the Aztecs of Mexico who saw the divinity only as a tyrannical and terrible power, and who were unable to conceive, like the Greeks and Hebrews, that the "gods, if they commit injustice, are no longer gods", generally succumbed in the struggle for existence, beneath the onslaught of rivals who were possibly no better than they, but for whom the heavens were not always hidden by storms and the wrath of sad and jealous gods.

III

THE CENTURY OF MAGO

For six and a half centuries a small group of Phœnicians, cast up on an unproductive and barbarous coast, and soon to be deprived of all material help from the metropolis, surrounded by enemies and rivals, succeeded in maintaining the astonishing Western maritime and commercial empire which Tyre had entrusted to their custody. Furthermore, when Tyre itself had abandoned national traditions, even to the extent of forgetting its own language, the Carthaginians of Africa remained obstinately attached to them, spread them further and, even after Carthage itself had been razed to the ground, assured their survival to the end of antiquity. This task required astonishing qualities of energy, tenacity, intelligence and courage, the very qualities incarnated in Hannibal, the greatest of all Carthaginians and the only one whose personality is known. It might easily be thought that this task was made possible by a creative genius similar to that of the Egyptians, Hebrews or Greeks, which, in giving birth to a powerful and original civilisation, animated by full confidence in its spiritual ideals, finds the strength to resist defeat and to spread the enthusiasm by which it is inspired, amongst barbarians. However, this was not at all the case. In the realms of knowledge, art, even technique, Carthage created nothing of its own and it bequeathed nothing which survived it. Its contribution to human civilisation is certainly less than that of some completely barbarous peoples, such as the Gauls.

The poverty of information must be regretted, particularly the almost complete lack of all evidence by Carthaginians about themselves. Apart from the tale of the adventures of Hanno, preserved by the Greeks because of its picturesque quality, no Punic written work of any extent has survived. However, this is not because none existed. Even after the conflagrations, Scipio found entire libraries intact and allowed the Numidian kings to put the contents into safe keeping. Unfortunately, these works were not translated, except the famous Treatise of Agronomy by Mago, and the Africans, overcome by Greco-Latin culture, soon ceased to copy and even to read them. Thus, the irony of fate has decreed that nothing be known of the more recent Phœnician literature, though texts have been found which were

[11] A sixth century tomb built up with blocks sloping outwards from the entrance lintel.

[12] Interior of a tomb. Two sarcophagi, made of limestone slabs from El Haouaria, are visible.

Page 41

[13] Cippus in the shape of a throne, in limestone from El Haouaria. The god is represented by the central pillar. The inscription is one of the rare texts from Carthage which is earlier than the fifth century. The first line can be translated as: cippus offered for a Molk sacrifice, to Ba'al. This word Molk, wrongly interpreted, has been taken for that of a god, Moloch. The throne symbolises the majesty of the god, and is sometimes worshipped empty. Tanit is not named on this monument. Compare it with the Phoenician cippus: G. Contenau, *Man. d'Arch. Orient.*, III, p.1472, fig. 892.

[14] Terra cotta statuette from the tophet. Sixth century B.C. archaic style idol, reproducing a hermaphrodite fertility god.

[15] Baitulos. This word is the Greek transcription of a Phoenician expression which literally means "the house of the god". The stone—a pebble from a volcanic rock—was considered to harbour a supernatural power because of its hardness and regular shape. To express this belief a face has been roughly engraved on it, with bestial features which express the terrible force of Ba'al.

[16] Egyptian amulets. The Carthaginians were very superstitious and always had a predilection for Egyptian amulets. Egyptian priests had a reputation for excelling in the occult arts. Notice on Nos. 9 and 13 two scarabs: the lower side, which was used as a seal, has been photographed to show the relief. No. 13 represents the god Bes (see Ill. 19). The scarabs were first imported into Carthage from Egypt, notably from the Greek town of Naucratis. After the fifth century, they were manufactured in Sardinia, in jasper. In the fourth century and later, their decoration was often of Greek inspiration (see Ill. 58). They were worn on the breast, hanging on a cord from the ring around which they pivoted, or as a ring on the finger.

Nos. 5 and 8: Pendants reproducing the Egyptian sign of life, the *ankh*. This symbol resembles the sign of Tanit, with which it has been confused.

Nos. 1, 2 and 3: Amulet-holding tubes. They contained a parchment or a leaf of precious metal engraved with magic signs. The animal head at the top of the tube represents a god: for the ram, see also Ill. 18. Above the head of the lion on Tube 1, note the erect cobra in front of the sphere symbolising the sun.

The other objects shown on this plate are jewels: earrings (No. 10) or buckles (14, 15). Notice the chasing on the jewel No. 5; this technique was particularly developed in Etruria.

[17] Stele from the tophet at Sousse: goddess (Tanit?) whose
head-dress is reminiscent of the crown of Upper Egypt. There is
a perfume-pan in front of her. Notice the "withered" arm holding
a sphere. Fifth century B.C.

Nos. 17 to 20 illustrate Egyptian influence at Carthage, particularly in the religious sphere. This influence reached its height in the seventh and sixth centuries, but persisted till the end of Carthage.

[18] Small terra cotta head (here enlarged about three times) representing the sacred ram. This creature, consecrated to Ammon in Egypt, was the object of a cult with the Libyans of Algeria from the prehistoric period. But the connections that have been believed to exist between these two centres do not seem to have been proven. At Carthage, Ammon was assimilated to Ba'al Hammon. The ram often appeared on steles. Compare also the head from the amulet-holding tubes (Ill. 16, No. 3). Third century B.C.

[19] Large ivory amulet representing the god Bes. This god, Egyptian in origin, but adopted early by the Phoenicians, and represented as a dwarf, chased away evil forces by his very ugliness, and overthrew them.

[20] Fragment from a stele covered with hieroglyphic inscriptions and representing the god Horus walking on crocodiles. These small monuments gave protection from bites by poisonous animals.

committed by the scribes of Ugarit to indestructible clay tablets in the fourteenth century B.C. The most important intellectual progress achieved by the Phœnicians itself contributed to this catastrophe. The people of Ugarit already used an alphabet, but one formed of cuneiform signs borrowed from Mesopotamia, requiring the use of a tablet and metallic stylus. When the alphabet, which is the ancestor of our own, became prevalent, the brick—which was imperishable but too heavy—was replaced by papyrus. Since then only monumental texts engraved on stone have escaped the ravages of time.[1]

Phœnician inscriptions engraved on stone certainly exist in Africa by the thousand. Since the end of the last century, French Semitists, at first directed by E. Renan, have carefully garnered them in the *Corpus Inscriptionum Semiticarum*. But these documents give the same misleading impression as so many other products of Punic civilisation, firstly because of their relatively late date; only two or three go further back than the fifth century B.C. Even more regrettable is the almost complete lack of interest of the votive inscriptions from the *tophet*, or of the epitaphs which form nearly the whole body of the collection. The longest texts have some religious value in themselves. These are two sacrificial schedules, instructive despite their dryness, and some sanctuary dedications, mixed with imprecations. By comparison, the great neo-Punic inscriptions, that is to say, written after the destruction of Carthage, found in Tripolitania and in some towns of Numidia, seem like treasures. Unfortunately, the writing, so deformed that some of the letters are almost indistinguishable from one another, is much more difficult to decipher as the vowels are not marked nor the words separated. Even the language is not easy to follow because Phœnician is translated with the aid of Hebrew, which it greatly resembles, without however being identical. When a serious divergence between the two languages appears, the philologist has to strain his ingenuity without always reaching definite results. Thus the formula NSB MLKT BMSRM, which Renan understood as "the Prefect of the Queen in Egypt" is today translated as "stele offered in the place of his flesh" by J. G. Février.

The poor quality of the Punic epitaphs arouses doubt as to the value of its extinct literature. If Roman thought were only known through African epigraphy, the discovery of some Virgilian cento, or some quotation from Ennius in an epitaph or mosaic would still make it possible to envisage the existence of Latin poetry. Nothing in the inexorable dryness of the vows engraved on the steles of the *tophet*

---

[1]Clay seals have been discovered at Carthage, which sealed the rolls of papyrus. They are all that remain of a library which was burned, dating from the fourth century B.C.

gives rise to the supposition that the fanatical Punic religion ever inspired a poet. The poetic verve which gave birth to those strange epics
at Ugarit, sometimes reminiscent in tone of the Bible and sometimes
of Hesiod, could not have survived in the West. Only the texts
translated into Latin and of very late date show a breath of real
emotion, some small part of the sacred terror of Ba'al and his *molk*:
"That this act be good, agreeable to the gods and beneficial. To the
Holy Lord, Saturn, great sacrifice of night, molchomor; spirit for
spirit, blood for blood, life for life. N. has accomplished it for the
well-being of N. following a vow, at the order of God, after having
seen his face. A lamb was the substitute."

Some pompous titles translated into Latin in Tripolitanian inscriptions—*amator civium* and *ornator patriae*—suggest an ostentatious and
heavy public eloquence. From this style Tertullian and the African
rhetors may have borrowed, more by atavism than by conscious
imitation, those of their effects which modern standards of taste find
most dubious.

The evidence of the monuments partly supplements the lack of
texts. Flaubert, writing *Salammbô*, had to imagine the whole human
framework from purely literary documentation. By a veritable *tour
de force* he succeeded in evoking objects without describing them.
Today, the Lavigerie Museum at Carthage and the Alaoui Museum
at le Bardo exhibit objects found in several thousand Carthaginian
tombs. But these collections, to which all classes of the population
and all periods of life at Carthage have contributed, eloquently pro-
claim the sterility of its civilisation. The following rule can be formulated, and exceptions to it are rare: every object of value was imported;
every object manufactured at Carthage was of mediocre quality.
Elegant pottery modelled at Corinth, painted with real or imaginary
animals, warriors, chariots and riders, with a thousand rosettes or
palmettes, stands next to heavy two-handled Punic vases, scarcely
enhanced by a few red lines on a light base. Glass scarabs from
Egypt, those from Sardinia cut from jasper, and terra cotta figurines
bought from the Greeks of Sicily, put to shame the crude Carthaginian
ware which tried to imitate them after a fashion. It can even be said
that techniques imported into Carthage, far from developing there,
regularly degenerated. "The artistic gifts of a people," writes S. Gsell,
"reveal themselves in the most everyday things: but these attest to
the irremediable impotence of the Carthaginians. They could not even
imitate their Greek models skilfully; in this respect, they were very
inferior to the Etruscans, copyists like themselves . . . The Carthaginians had no illusions as to the value of their industry: when they

wanted some piece that was not too vulgar, they obtained it abroad."
This is a far cry from the luxurious and refined civilisation it pleased
Flaubert to imagine. How disappointed he would have felt if he had
known that the Palace of Hamilcar undoubtedly resembled some
bourgeois Levantine interior, overloaded with knick-knacks from
bazaars, rough tapestries and crude imitations of Eastern carpets.

This low standard of techniques often confuses the archæologist
when he classifies and dates the objects discovered, and also increases
the obscurity surrounding Carthage. The specialist in Greek ceramics
finds a thousand indications in the rich decoration of his vases, to
enable him to group them into families, from which by comparison he
then determines origin and age. He can thus succeed in dating to
within ten or twenty years the activity of some Corinthian or Athenian
workshop of the sixth or fifth century B.C. The "Punicologist" can
only envy him when faced with his crude pottery, the evolution of
which is only vaguely marked by a progressive degeneration of form.
The absolute chronology of Carthaginian industry can mainly be
determined by the simultaneous discovery of its products and imported pieces. In the *tophet*, the votive deposits, which were never
removed, have remained superposed in layers, each of which corresponds to one period, the lowest naturally being the oldest. The
excavator therefore endeavours to measure the position of each object
most carefully along three co-ordinates. This is the stratigraphic
method borrowed from the prehistorians; it gives good results, so
long as the possibility of the "slipping" of more recent objects into a
lower layer is taken into account. Prehistorians were also the first to
try to date an object by physical and chemical analysis. After examin-
ing the earth to determine its organic composition and density—
which sometimes enables pottery workshops to be located—P. Cintas
moved on to a new method which should be able to yield dates with
mathematical precision. The magnetic field of the earth is known to
be subject to regular variations, rising and declining, which can be
traced on a graph and which follow a sinusoid curve. Meanwhile,
physicists have discovered that ceramics, because they contain minute
crystals of iron, behave like true magnets, naturally of an infinitesimal
power, and that they have a field identical to that of the earth. Most
important, this magnetic field has been fixed—fossilised, to use the
happy expression of E. Thellier—in each of these minute magnets at
the moment of firing. It follows from this that if the date of a piece of
pottery and its place of origin is known, the magnetic incline at that
date can be measured. Conversely, if all the values taken in the course
of time by this incline are known, the pottery, on condition that its

Large mausoleum, preceded by a smoking altar; in front of it, a cock, the victim offered to the dead.

Decoration painted on the walls of a tomb at Jbel Mlezza (Cape Bon).

A fortified town with houses of several storeys. In a niche beside it, the sign of Tanit.

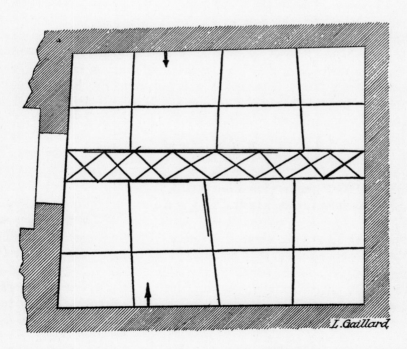

Decoration painted on the walls of a tomb at Jbel Mlezza (Cape Bon).

place of manufacture be known, can be dated. Results obtained in recent years give hope that the ballistic galvanometer may become a normal instrument of archæological research. Furthermore, the results of this method can be combined with other physical processes. Thus, organic matter contains an isotope radioactive with carbon, Carbon 14, the destruction of which takes place according to a regular process.

Modern archæologists, armed with the most precise techniques, heedful of the slightest indication, are very different from the hunters for rare objects who plundered ancient deposits scarcely more than a century ago. It must however be regretted that many amateurs, more or less disinterested, or even semi-scholars, badly equipped or over-hasty, have often irremediably spoiled the richest sites even at Carthage, and in Cape Bon. The majority of tombs have been explored without sufficient precautions. The scrupulous methods of P. Gauckler, Director of Antiquities at Tunis at the beginning of the century, were unfortunately not those of all his contemporaries. Even today, despite strict legislation, clandestine excavations still go on and profit too often from the indulgence of public opinion. It must be hoped that the present very general interest in the science of the past will put an end to practices which, for the selfish satisfaction of a few people, deprive all humanity of the most precious teachings of its past.

Agatha Christie, the wife of an Assyriologist, once defined the archæologist as a detective of the past. In this case, acting as a true blood-hound, he strains his ingenuity to draw the most valuable information from such a reticent and stupid witness as the tedious industry of Carthage. Meanwhile, the historian, the honest judge, overcomes the dislike which it inspires in him in order to question himself on the causes of its downfall.

The Semitic peoples in general have little gift for the plastic arts. The Hebrews at least had the virtue of refusing to enter the field at all, the Arabs that of developing an abstract decoration conforming to the austerity of their beliefs. The Phœnicians, those of Africa particularly, simply floundered in bad taste. They were undoubtedly encouraged in this by economic conditions: they were working for an extensive and unrefined clientèle, whom they cheated by swopping their shoddy goods for very valuable raw materials. But the need to concentrate all energies in order to ensure the survival of the community may also have stifled cultural activity, and their jealous attachment to national and religious tradition may have engendered an intolerance towards all novelties suspected of spoiling its purity. Ethnic minorities in the midst of foreigners are very often found to persist, particularly in the Orient, largely as a result of their uncompromising faithfulness to a very old religion and of the economic power of their members, who apply themselves to business matters with an intelligence restrained in all other matters by a rigid conservatism. Unlike the Parsees, Armenians or Kharedjites of the present-day Maghreb, the Carthaginians were able to preserve their political independence and economic power for a long time. But at least for the last three centuries of their history—those we know best—they were encircled by ruthless enemies, either natives or colonists of other races, who reduced them to the verge of despair on more than one occasion. It is therefore tempting to explain Punic "dullness of mind" by a sort of "ghetto complex", as Carthage seems suddenly to have retired within itself in order to survive, when the Greek menace was most threatening—in the fifth century B.C.

In fact, it would appear that the Carthage of the seventh and sixth centuries B.C. had not yet experienced hardship and sorrow. Unfortunately, only faint indications are available for the history of that important period, which enable a glimpse to be caught of a great effort both to impose the authority of the new Tyre on the other Phœnician colonies of Africa and Spain, by taking over the rôle of the metropolis in assisting them against native revolts, and to ensure control of Mediterranean routes to the West. The occupation of Sardinia and the Balearics, undoubtedly achieved in the seventh century B.C., guaranteed the Punic fleets mastery of the high seas. But the Greeks had already occupied the coasts of eastern Sicily, only leaving the Phœnicians the western point of the island, where the Elymi who may have been of Asiatic origin, opened Eryx, Drepana, Segesta and Palnormus to them. At the beginning of the sixth century B.C., the Ionians occupied in Marseilles a key position which made coastwise trade along the Provençal coasts towards Catalonia impossible for Punic vessels, and deprived them of the great commercial outlet of the Rhône. The savagery of the Celtic tribes and the continual troubles disturbing central and northern Gaul rendered this approach to the tin mines of Great Britain and the amber of the Baltic more hazardous than the route over the Alpine passes, then controlled by the Etruscans, or the old maritime way along the Atlantic coasts where Carthage was unchallenged. Etruscans and Carthaginians may have competed at first, but they quickly realised that self-interest demanded union against the Greeks. This was sealed in 536 B.C., when the Phocæans, the founders of Marseilles, were driven from their city by Crœsus and attempted to occupy Corsica en masse. If their enterprise had succeeded, Italy would have been denied access to Africa. The combined fleets of the two powers put an end to the threat at Alalia and this success helped to stabilise the alliance. Very precise treaties defined the zones of respective influence, which furthermore complemented each other perfectly. The Etruscans, then at the summit of their power, had almost unified Italy, from the Alps to Campania. The coasts of eastern Sicily and southern Italy, just transformed by colonisation into Magna Græcia, were thus enclosed in a vice formed by the north of the peninsula, Sardinia, eastern Sicily and Africa. The *entente* between the Etruscans and the Carthaginians even extended to economic and cultural relations: statuettes, Etruscan pottery and some inscriptions in the Tyrrhenian language have been discovered at Carthage. Above all, one of the mysterious Carthaginian sarcophagi containing a statue—which will be mentioned later—has its exact equivalent at Tarquinia, which points to a certain similarity of eschatological beliefs between the two peoples.

The Tyrrheno-Punic alliance extended into the West the coalition of all the Eastern nations which had been formed by the Persian conquest. The collapse of the Assyrian empire in 612 B.C. brought no perceptible relief to Phœnicia. Far from profiting from the rivalry between the new Babylonian empire and Egypt, it was exposed to attacks from both sides. Tyre in particular was blockaded for thirteen years by Nebuchadnezzar after 587 B.C., and in resisting him exhausted the forces which Assurbanipal had been unable to destroy. The Persians, on the other hand, appeared in about 550 B.C. as liberators to all the peoples of Syria. These mountain-dwellers, to whom everything connected with the sea was foreign, but who were obliged to protect the coasts of their empire, treated the Lebanese sailors more as collaborators than as subjects. Tyre was undoubtedly too hard-hit and had to resign itself to yielding first place to its old rival, Sidon. Thenceforward, the prince of Sidon emerges as Admiral of the Great King. But this decadence did not reach her colony. On the contrary, the other Western Tyrian cities henceforth acknowledged a hegemony in Carthage, which they were reluctant to transfer to the Sidonians. Moreover, they could appear impartial in the defence of the common interests of the nation. When after conquering Egypt, Cambyses intended to direct an expedition against Carthage, the Phœnicians quite clearly opposed it. They declared, according to Herodotus, that it would be ungodly to make war on their children! Although the King scarcely ever permitted his wishes to be denied, he did not dare to go further because, the father of history adds, the army of the sea depended entirely on the Phœnicians. Moreover, Carthage wanted nothing better than to be a part of the Empire. At times she even allowed the Persians to inspect her mysterious trading stations in Morocco. The embassy which solemnly bore the colony's tribute to the Melqart of Tyre certainly received more temporal instructions side by side with its pious mission. The principal object of these conversations was obviously the struggle against the Greeks.

The great conflict between the Persian empire and the Hellenic must to a large extent have been provoked by the intrigues of the Phœnicians, who glimpsed a means of destroying their most dangerous competitors. The occupation of the coast of Asia Minor by the Persian armies at the end of the sixth century B.C. had already destroyed the maritime power of Ionia. The Phœnicians established in the east of Cyprus had a considerable advantage over the Greeks. On all shores Hellenic merchants and colonists found themselves face to face with united adversaries, directly commanded by or closely linked with their Lebanese rivals.

Carthage was naturally the central target: first in Sicily, where it had to relinquish the defence of the old Phœnician trading-posts grouped along the eastern coasts. Here, however, strengthened by the support of the Elymi, it concentrated its armies in fortresses on the western tip of the island in case of a counter-offensive. In Libya, it could not prevent the Dorians from occupying Cyrenaica, but it stopped them at the base of the Gulf of Syrtes. Particularly in the western basin, as already seen, it drove the Phocæans from Corsica and finally put an end to Greek attempts to link up directly with Tartessos.

Necessity had forced Carthage to become a military power. By nature the Phœnicians were sailors or merchants and did not like war. They were, however, capable of heroism, and the contempt in which they held their lives astonished the Greeks. Sallust describes a memorable act, reminiscent of the heroic legends of ancient Rome: the Punics and Cyrenians, after some indecisive battles, decided to fix their frontier at a point where two teams of runners who had set out from the most remote town in either territory, would meet. The champions of the Carthaginians, two brothers called the Philæni, succeeded in covering the greater distance. The Greeks disputed the validity of the performance. The Philæni then declared that they were prepared to be buried alive at the site of their victory on condition that their country retained its advantage. Their self-sacrifice was accepted. Until the end of antiquity, the altars of the Philæni on the coast of the Syrtes marked the extreme limit of Hellenism. This gloomy story may not be a legend. The souls of the tortured men buried in the earth seemed to be transformed into an immortal and ferocious spirit which refused to allow defeat. Such men as these, pitiless to themselves, could not be humane to their enemies. The cruelty of the Carthaginians in the destruction of captured towns, the massacres of large numbers of prisoners and the refined tortures inflicted on others, may have been exaggerated by Greek historians but not invented from nothing. Moreover, archæology has found traces of the destruction wrought by the Punic armies in Sicily. These acts of violence to which the Greeks recklessly replied gave birth to a ferocious hatred between the two races.

But Carthage, while capable of waging a vigorous war against the Greeks, does not seem to have understood the economic danger they presented in the seventh and sixth centuries B.C. The wars did not prevent commerce between the nations; the number of Greek objects discovered in Punic necropolises bears eloquent witness to this. There are firstly ceramics, primarily manufactured at Corinth. These are decorated in black on a red or white base with innumerable designs, still inspired by Eastern art and not yet imbued with the sober spirit that Athens was to impose in the following century. These vases were not only valuable in themselves. Many of them contained precious products, particularly perfume. *Objets d'art*, statuettes, masks, jewels and bronzes were also of Greek origin. These products of Hellenic industry formed the major part of Carthage's imports at this period. Undoubtedly Etruria, even Phœnicia and Egypt, also sent their manufactured objects, but some scholars think that the Greeks also served as agents in trade with Egypt. In any case, scarabs manufactured in the Ionian town of Naucratis, founded in 630 B.C., on the coast of the Delta, certainly exist in great numbers amongst the objects found. Yet Phœnician and particularly Carthaginian products are almost entirely absent from Greece and even from Italy at this period. This shows that from the sixth century B.C. onwards a grave threat was hanging over the still prosperous economy of the new Tyre—which, it will be remembered, had been founded to control the transport of raw materials of Western origin to the East, and to exchange them for the products of Levantine industry. In fact, the Phœnicians were unable to prevent their principal rivals from intruding on this traffic. It is certain that quite a large amount of trade was still carried on between Africa and Lebanon by way of Cyprus, which belonged to the Persian empire. But these cargoes had to cross seas infested with Greek pirates. On the other hand, the troubles in the East in the seventh century B.C. had brought about a decline of the Phœnician and Egyptian industries which was to the advantage of Greece; henceforth no civilised country could afford not to trade with her. The Persian unification of Asia had finally facilitated the transport of supplies to the great human agglomerations of the fertile plains by overland routes, thus reducing their dependence on the West. The route from Tarshish therefore lost much of the importance it had possessed at the time of Hiram I and Solomon. Its decline can be dated according to a theory put forward by P. Cintas: until the beginning of the sixth century B.C., Carthage used heavy ceramics manufactured at Tyre. At that date, these were replaced by vases manufactured on the spot. But the importing of heavy jars of little value is only understandable if they served as homeward bound freight in the vessels which brought minerals from Tarshish to the east. They therefore ceased to circulate in the first half of the sixth century B.C. But the Carthaginian leaders do not seem to have realised the danger. They continued to allow the purchase of luxury products from the Greeks and in exchange had to give up a considerable part of the metals collected at great expense in the West. Furthermore, they had not succeeded in developing an industry at Carthage capable of competing with the Greeks—the Etruscans on the contrary were able to do this. The Carthaginians were content to produce shoddy goods with which the savages of the north or the negroes were obliged to be satisfied, as a result of the mercantile policy forcibly imposed on them.

Available information, unfortunately very fragmentary, does moreover show that the political régime had not yet acquired the stability and rigorous authority which later assured the safety of Carthage. The Greeks named the chiefs with whom they had dealings in Sicily, kings—*basileis*. Justin calls one of them Malchus, which is only the royal title in the Semitic languages (*melek*). He may have confused the name of the function with that of the man. It is not known whether the kings of Carthage were legitimately connected with the dynasty of Dido or whether they were usurpers like the Greek "tyrants"— which would appear more probable. Whatever the origin of their power, even the story of Malchus shows that they were not absolute. Returning from war in Sicily, this prince wanted to change the form of government. The Senate opposed his projects and the city closed its doors on him. Even the son of Malchus, Carthalon, who belonged to the priesthood of Melqart and had just led the sacred embassy to Tyre, refused to support his father. The king then laid siege to Carthage. Carthalon decided to go to his father's camp in the hope of winning him over. Malchus had his son crucified, still wearing his pontifical costume. Undoubtedly he hoped to move the heavens to mercy by sacrificing a doubly precious victim: precious both as the son of the king and as a priest. According to Punic theology, priestly consecration put the life of the *cohen* in the hands of the god, who could, in principle, reclaim it at any time. However, Malchus was unable to achieve his ambitions and soon met a violent death. Power then passed to the family of the Magonids, who retained it for at least three generations, at the end of the sixth and the beginning of the fifth centuries.

Some idea of the public monuments of Carthage can be obtained from the cippi of the *tophet*. Some show miniature temples, the architecture of which is purely Egyptian. Massive doors framed with straight pillars are surmounted by concave cornices known as Egyptian grooves. The frieze is often decorated with erect cobras or a winged disc, the symbol of Amon Ra. Ever since the third millennium, the Phœnicians had been in the habit of copying Pharaonic buildings in simplified form. The Carthaginians kept up this tendency by imitating monuments from their native land, not by borrowing directly. Their negligence soon caused the style to degenerate, but the technique of construction remained good. It can be judged from the tombs of this period; vaults constructed of large blocks of sandstone, fitted without cement. The walls were often covered with a layer of fine stucco. A cedar-wood ceiling masked the stone roof, formed of two rows of blocks shored up to form a ridge-roof. After exhausting the quarries on the peninsula, the Carthaginians opened much more extensive ones at the extremity of Cape Bon. Immense shafts were sunk in the beds of limestone there. These prison-quarries, less well-known but quite as impressive as those of Syracuse, opened directly on to the sea so that the slaves employed there could not flee into the country, and cargo ships could come directly to the exit of the quarry to load the stone for transportation to the other side of the gulf. But this flaky, coarse-textured limestone scarcely lent itself to carving. The primitiveness of Punic sculpture is to a large extent the result of the mediocrity of the material, which the artists tried to improve with stucco covering. Unbaked bricks were also used for less important constructions. Some tombs at Utica are thus simply built of clay; only the grave stone itself is a block of sandstone.

Religion, like political organisation, had not yet taken final shape. Two inscriptions of this period engraved on the cippi of the *tophet* are dedicated to Ba'al alone. Tanit was therefore not yet Queen of Carthage. It is not known whether Ba'al already was surnamed Hammon. However, he was only the chief of a complex pantheon. A goddess was certainly associated with him as paredros. He was the master of the *tophet*, but other gods—Melqart was the most venerated —also had temples in the city. The people were not very anxious to represent them in human form, just as they hesitated to call them by their true names, because the divine power appeared so fearful that it would strike down anyone so imprudent as to come into contact with it. On the *tophet*, Ba'al was usually represented by a simple pillar of rectangular stone, often placed on a throne, to symbolise his fearful majesty, or sheltered within a miniature chapel. The pillar was often divided into two or three. It then represented the god with his paredros, or surrounded by advisers who served him as ministers. The sacred energy was also represented in round pebbles of hard rock on which a bestial face was roughly carved. The principal natural manifestation of the god was the sun. Its disc, decorated with wings in the Egyptian style, was often engraved on the façade of the miniature temple which frequently sheltered its symbol.

Egyptian theology still exercised a profound influence and a number of symbols, together with some divine figures, were borrowed from it. These include the sacred *najas* or cobras which decorate the friezes of the chapels, and mysterious figures shaped like mummies which can be glimpsed in the depths of their cella. The god also promoted fertility. Rough terra cotta statuettes represented male, female, even bi-sexual, personages, with exaggerated sexual attributes. The Punic religion may have had at this period a sensual character, which afterwards diminished.

Superstition played a more important part than religion in everyday life. The Carthaginian thought he was surrounded by innumerable forces, most frequently malevolent, from which he must protect himself all the time. He lived and died covered with amulets, possibly the most curious objects the civilisation produced. They were borrowed from everywhere, from every nation: the negro's cowrie which resembles a female sexual organ, and the Beduins' coarse leather square were certainly not despised. But the most efficient phylacteries came from Egypt, laden with all the prestige of the oldest and most religious of peoples. Almost all the gods of the Nile were represented: Hathor the good cow, Horus the sparrow-hawk, Bastit the cat, Anubis with the head of a jackal, Osiris, Isis with the infant Horus, Touaris the hippopotamus, and so on. Symbols or objects of worship included the *oudja* eye, which drove out the evil eye, the column Zed with its palmiform capital, the papyriform column Ouaz, the serpent Uræus. Gold or silver tubes topped by the head of the ram of Ammon, contained gold or silver leaves engraved with images of Egyptian gods and with a Punic inscription recommending the bearer to their protection.

Other Punic phylacteries, peculiar to the time, are famous. These are the terra cotta masks that are found particularly in tombs. Some represent a woman smiling, others show the face of a man quite similar to the contemporary Greek *kouroi*; the nostrils of one are pierced by a ring. Finally, there are grimacing masks, deformed by warts or strange tattooing. For a long time, these were thought to be portraits; they were even cited as the last remains of Punic realism. In fact, the models came from Greece and the masks themselves, or at least the moulds used to make them, were probably bought at Rhodes. Grimacing masks have been discovered at Sparta in the sanctuary of Artemis Orthia. This foreign origin excludes the possibility of their representing Carthaginians. But they certainly were images of supernatural beings: those with noble expressions were benevolent gods and goddesses; the others were grimacing demons, meant to frighten the evil spirits with an ugliness equal to their own, by virtue of the magic precept: *similia similibus curantur*. Actors may have worn them for sacred dances.

There is a complete lack of any information on private dwelling and costume in this period. On this last point, however, the persistence of Oriental styles, confirmed later, entitles us to imagine the Carthaginians, clad like their ancestors on the Assyrian or Egyptian monuments, in a long robe with sleeves, completed by a pointed cap. Funeral material has preserved a very large number of jewels: ear-rings, nose-rings, bracelets, necklaces often made up of amulets, and breast plates in the Egyptian style. From the Egyptians also came the custom of wearing a pottery or enamelled steatite scarab either on a ring or suspended from a cord around the neck. The underside of the object, which bore an Egyptian hieroglyphic inscription, could be used as a seal. To make it easier to use, the scarab pivoted around an axis which fixed it to its ring.

The survival of Oriental traditions appeared in the most humble objects, such as everyday pottery, which has been preserved in large quantities: the artisan, the small merchant, the cultivator had scarcely any furniture other than the large jars in which he not only stored provisions—grain, wine, oil—but often also the fabrics, and the poor jewels in which he invested his savings, as the Beduin of Tunisia still do. When night came, a bowl of oil with a wick gave them some sort of light in the raw brick huts. They cooked over a small brick stove, very similar to the present-day *kanoun*. Despite their weight, the jars even accompanied the sailor in his bark. "At first sight," writes P. Cintas, "it is hard to understand why a number of the jars, and some of the largest, end in a point or have an appendage at their base. Some of these could not have been stowed away on boats in any way other than that used for their present-day homologues on the Kerkenian barks. An opening in the bridge allows the jar to descend vertically into the hold. The mouth of the jar then coincides with the level of the bridge, from which it barely projects, and the tail fits into a hole made in one of the planks in the boat's hull just below the opening through which the jar descends. The jar is then held vertically without the least possibility of being displaced by the rolling. The sailor can dip into the contents of the jar, from the bridge itself, using a bowl. Other jars have a conical base which adapts them for use as "baskets" to be hung on the sides of pack animals. Even in our own days, throughout Tunisia, the water-carriers come to fill these same jars at the street fountains. They are transported on donkey-back with the help of a sort of double-bag made of reeds or osier (*cheria*) with pockets which hang on either side of the animals' flanks . . . The distribution of water was certainly no better organised in Punic times than today, and a number of terra cotta statuettes found in the tombs show the curious appearance of the horse carrying its load of water. This method has therefore been preserved until the present, because since antiquity nothing has modified the technique of transporting water from the spring or from wells to the house. But I believe that it will soon suddenly disappear. In the country, in all the area covered by the Afrika Korps or the Eighth Army, the pointed jars have today been replaced by unbreakable metal cans which the troops used to transport petrol and which they abandoned on their march. At the same time, the basket-makers ceased to manufacture their *cheria*, for it had become pointless."

The Carthaginians showed in the manufacture of these humble vases, the familiar instruments of their everyday life, an originality of which they were incapable in the creation of *objets d'art*. As long as trade with Tarshish lasted, the heavy jars manufactured at Tyre and piled up as freight on the boats bringing back minerals, were enough for the needs of Carthage. When the Punic workshops had to make good their absence, they progressively modified their shapes without, in general, being inspired by foreign models. Specialists distinguish the "native" forms from imported vases by simple details: the attachment of the handles, and the design of the neck and shoulders. Till the end, the Punics remained faithful to a lamp which worked on very simple principles, a bowl with its edges pinched to form one, and then, very soon afterwards, two lips. Only towards the middle of the fourth century B.C. were the edges raised to protect the reservoir of oil. But Greek lamps—imported in quite large numbers in an early period—can be distinguished at first glance by their closed circular reservoir and their tubular lip.

The choice of the most ordinary furniture undisguisedly reveals the spirit of the people. Luxury objects, sought for their rarity as much as their value, were often borrowed from foreign civilisations. The archæological legacy of seventh and sixth century Carthage therefore shows the continued survival of Phœnician modes of life, particularly remarkable because Canaanite civilisation was never distinguished for its powerful personality and because many of the colonists of the new Tyre were undoubtedly not themselves born in Lebanon. Faithfulness to tradition seemed to the Carthaginians the guarantee of the survival of their power. They turned the same energy to preserving it as to driving the Greek vessels far from the shores of Africa and Spain. Undoubtedly the time had passed when the powerful *gauloi* of Hiram, in their rounded hulks, brought to Tyre silver and tin from Europe, gold and ivory from Africa. The real clients of Carthage were no longer of the same race, but the Hellenes, their hated rivals, who were nevertheless admired for their skill in sculpturing marble, moulding bronze and painting the most insignificant little clay vase in a thousand precious colours. Their spirit of enterprise was mistrusted, their courage feared, but the Carthaginians reassured themselves with the thought of all the friendly nations which encircled the Greek ports and, above all, with the infinite power of the Great King. Advised by his Sidonian admiral, irritated by the turbulence of his new Ionian subjects, it is known that the latter planned to send his innumerable armies beyond the Hellespont and the Aegean. Carthage and her friends in Etruria would then only have to unite their forces once more to annihilate the Greeks of Italy and Sicily at the same time, and to re-establish an economic and naval hegemony from one end of the Mediterranean to the other which no one would ever have the power to overthrow.

[21] Large onyx jar, similar to the Canopus vases and certainly imported from Egypt (sixth century B.C.)

[22 and 23] Half-figures of smiling goddesses, possibly Tanit. The origin of these objects, peculiar to the sixth and beginning of the fifth centuries, is not certain. But they were obviously influenced by Greek art of the end of the sixth century. They were generally put into tombs to protect the dead.

[24] Mask of a man in the same style. Some of these wear earrings and one even a nose-ring.

[25] A bronze bust, presumed to be of Hannibal, discovered at Volubilis in Morocco. It probably belonged to the collection owned by King Juba II and is thought by some to be a portrait of this king. But the stylistic characteristics are those of the third to second centuries B.C. and the resemblance of the profile to Hannibal's coinage is striking.

[26] Coin of Hannibal struck at Carthagena in about 220. A portrait of the young general in the likeness of Melqart-Heracles, as his father was shown. At that time he was slightly over twenty years old.

[27] Posthumous portrait of Hamilcar on a coin struck at Carthagena by Hannibal in 220. The Punic general is likened to Melqart-Heracles by the club also represented. (These coins were identified by E.S.G. Robinson.)

[28] Coin-portrait of Hasdrubal. This coin is a few years earlier than the preceding one. Hasdrubal wears a diadem, a confirmation of his pretensions to royalty, attested to by the historians.

[29] Everyday Punic ceramics.

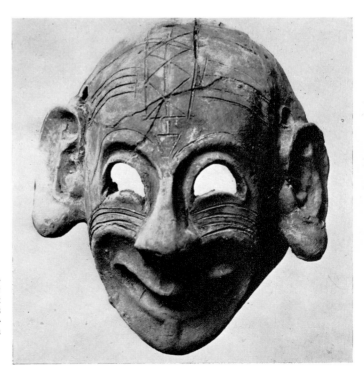

[30] Grimacing mask. It undoubtedly represents a demon. Exactly
similar masks have been found at
Sparta. They may reproduce masks
used for dances, when the partici-
pants identified themselves with
supernatural beings.

[31] The large vase in this plate was photographed in the garden at the Museum of Utica. "No one is proud of this ceramic, not even the men who produced it" (P. Cintas, *Céramique punique*, p. 518).

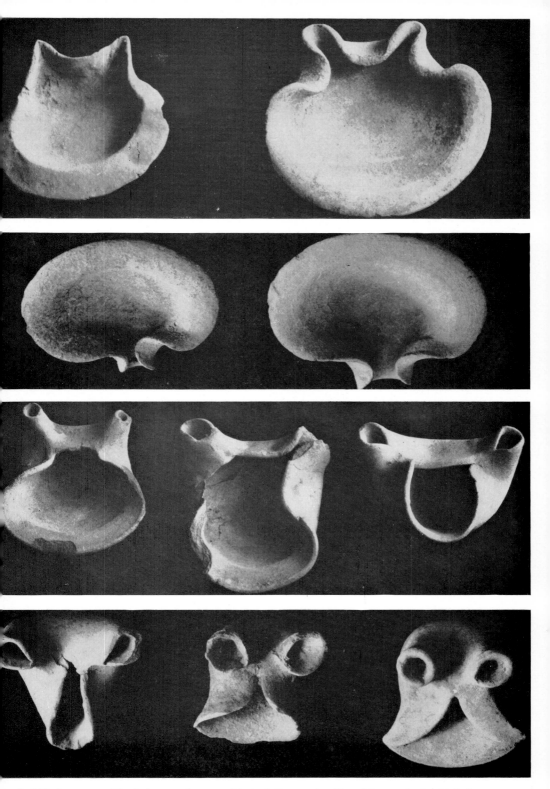

[32] Various types of Punic lamps. The ones with single lips are the oldest. The ones in the third picture, showing how the lamp tended to close up, come from the third century, those in the fourth from the second century.

[36] Stele in the shape of the "sign of Tanit" and engraved with the "sign of the bottle". Below is the dedication to Tanit and Ba'al Hammon which appeared on thousands of models.

[33 and 34] Primitive types of Punic ceramics. The first picture represents the oldest forms, imported for a long time from Tyre. The vase without a handle in the middle of the second picture is characteristic of the lowest levels of the tophet.

[35] Ass or horse water-carriers.

[37]

[39]

[38]

[37, 38 and 39] Types of stele: note the hand of the god on the fronton of stele 37 and his ears on the acroterium. Notice also the decoration of Ionic capitals. Below the inscription are scissors and a rudder. It will be noticed that this is shaped like a stern-post rudder. In Ill. 38 there is the ram, and in Ill. 39 below the dedication appear the divine hand, the sign of Tanit, and the Caduceus.

[40] Ceramic statuette from the Neo-Punic sanctuary of Thinissut: first century A.D. Notice the evolution of style under Classic influence; the head-dress here is a crown of feathers, of Mesopotamian origin. The sphinxes are female; their breasts symbolise fertility. The braces crossed over their chests are often worn by the Great Goddess. Notice the Hellenistic style of these monsters. The cult statue of Ba'al Hammon at Hadrumetum was still being reproduced on the money of the Emperor Claudius Albinus, a native of this town, at the end of the second century A.D.

[41] Funerary statue from the necropolis of Santa Monica (third century B.C.), showing how archaism persisted in Punic sculpture. Notice the rendering of the eyes and beard. Compare it with the mask in Ill. 24 and note the degeneration from the prototype. For the survival or archaism see also the mausoleum of Dougga in Ill. 86.

[42] This illustration and the ones following show the agricultural development of Africa. In the absence of documents from the Punic period, Roman monuments have been used. See also Ill. 80.

Ill. 42 reproduces a mosaic from Oudna (second century A.D.) showing a large estate in the plain of Oued Miliane, some 25 miles to the south of Carthage. The centre of the estate is situated in the fertile, though somewhat arid plain. (Note the well worked by a pump-handle.) Grain was cultivated here and sheep reared. The partridge was hunted with the aid of a hoop-net; the hunter was hidden under a goat skin and beat up the birds. The surrounding country extends over a region of hills, suitable for cultivating olives and rearing animals, and frequented by large game (panthers and wild boar).

[43] Ruins of presses in the plain. The olive tree grows wild in North Africa. Its cultivation was introduced by the Carthaginians in the coastal zone but spread to the interior in the second century B.C. (*Photo Combès*).

[44] Olive trees near a Roman triumphal arch, at Musti (Central Tunisia). (*Photo Combès*).

[45] Ostrich hunt, on a Roman mosaic from the third century A.D. The ostrich lived in North Africa until the end of the last century. The scene depicted here is of a pen, to which the captured birds have been brought.

IV

REVOLUTION AND REFORM (480-306 B.C.)

THE wars with the Medes are usually considered as the rising of the Greek cities against the menace of the Persian tyrant. What they were in fact was a movement of far greater extent, which simultaneously and on all fronts broke the encirclement with which the Hellenic world was threatened and, on the political plane, brought about the Greek annexation of the Mediterranean, prepared for over a century by the superiority of their industry and commercial methods. The Ancients themselves emphasised the fact that the battles of Salamis and Himera, when the tyrants, Gelon of Syracuse and Theron of Agrigentum crushed the armies of Hamilcar, the Magonid, took place on the same day. September 481 B.C. saw the most disastrous train of events ever known by eastern or western Phœnicians. The Sicilians complacently enumerated the losses of the combatants at 35 to 40,000 men massacred, several hundreds of boats destroyed, 2,773 kilogrammes of gold taken from the camp—to which must be added a war indemnity of 2,000 talents of silver. Such losses would have been serious enough to compromise the equilibrium of the Carthaginian economy, even if they had not been followed by indirect reverses of at least equal gravity. According to Herodotus, the Phœnicians had equipped three hundred ships, a quarter of the whole fleet, for Xerxes' expedition under the command of Tetramnestos of Sidon, Mattan, the son of Hiram of Tyre, and Merbal, the son of Agbal of Arad. While Persian admirals controlled the Ionian and Egyptian squadrons, rightly judged not very reliable, the Phœnicians, who were considered, according to Herodotus, the best sailors of the Empire, seem to have been directly under royal command. They paid dearly for this honour. Placed on the right wing, facing the Athenians, the vessels broke to pieces on the reef of Psytalleia. Xerxes, in his disappointment, ordered the execution of the commanders, who in turn tried in vain to put the responsibility on the Ionians. Events at the Eurymedon (468) were even worse. Here, Cimon captured the whole Phœnician squadron of eighty ships at one go. This triumph opened up the Cyprus route to the Athenian fleet; it installed itself there permanently, easily blockading the Lebanese coast. The situation

8

became graver still eight years later, when the Egyptian revolt against the Persians enabled the Athenians to assume control of the Delta. Henceforth, for the first time for a millennium, Phœnician vessels were shut up in their roads. In the same period, the Etruscans, the principal western allies of Carthage, saw their empire collapse. In 510 B.C., the Roman revolution had caused them to lose control of Latium. In 474 B.C., Syracuse and Cumae destroyed the Tyrrhenian fleet, and Campania, isolated, soon succumbed to the Samnites.

One generation had seen the collapse of the formidable coalition, of which Carthage had been one of the principals. Certainly its own realm had not been touched. The Greeks had not dared to venture to the west of Sardinia or along the coasts of Africa or Spain. But how long could this security last? If one Greek city succeeded in imposing lasting authority on the others, and particularly if this hegemony should be exercised by the strongest maritime city, Athens, would it allow itself to be denied a quarter of the seas? Already its most ambitious and persuasive councillors, first Themistocles and later Alcibiades, were encouraging the citizens to include the west in their political horizon. In 415 B.C., Alcibiades conceived the grandiose plan, even better than the defeat of Sparta, to assure his native land the superiority that Pericles had not been able to guarantee it: the conquest of Sicily, as a prelude to the domination of the whole western Mediterranean. The discourse which Thucydides attributed to the Syracusan politician, Hermocrates, shows the Carthaginians perfectly conscious of this menace and ready to face it. Still other dangers were added to the Greek menace. The Libyans, whom Malchus had conquered and forced to renounce the tribute that they had been receiving since the time of Dido, took up arms again when they saw that Carthage was beaten. It had to resign itself to resuming payment.

The political ability of the Punic leaders can best be seen in the intelligence with which they understood the danger and discovered its deep-seated causes and the means of remedying them. They also deserve unstinted praise for the ferocious energy with which they put their plans into action, without caring about the heavy sacrifices imposed on the citizens. For this period particularly, the historian regrets that the evolution of Carthage was not described by a Thucydides or a Polybius. The data which literary tradition supplies on the great Carthaginian revolution are in fact so fragmentary that the importance of the revolution would almost completely escape notice if it were not complemented by archæological evidence.

The first consequence of the defeat at Himera and the misfortunes which ensued was the ruin of the Magonids. "As this so powerful family", says Justin, "were a heavy weight on public liberty and controlled both the government and the judicature, a hundred judges chosen from amongst the senators were instituted. After each war, the generals had to account for their actions before this tribunal. Thus fear of the laws and judgments to which they would be submitted at Carthage would inspire them with respect for the authority of the State during their command." The principal members of the dynasty, Hanno and Gisco, were exiled. It is possible that the title of the supreme magistrature might then have been changed from king (*melek*) to judge (*shofat*, which the Latins have made into suffete), and its duration reduced. In any case, for that time and several centuries afterwards the institution of the Court of a Hundred assured the preponderance of the aristocracy at Carthage. Aristotle compares them to the Ephors of Lacedæmon, drawing their power, less from definite attributes, than from the absolute control they exercised over everyone, from the king to the least of the citizens or even the slaves. Again, according to Aristotle, the Hundred were assisted by numerous committees of five members, recruited by co-option. It can be conjectured that these were some type of specialised senatorial commissions, which finished by dispossessing the general assembly of most of its powers. It is a natural tendency of aristocracies to reserve authority to restricted bodies, deliberating in secret. The Carthaginian oligarchy also shared with similar régimes a suspicious anti-individualism. The anecdotes in which the ancient moralists delight, complacently describe the disgrace of important personages, particularly generals, whose loyalty was suspected or whose enterprises were unlucky. Several died under refined tortures. In ancient societies, where civilised organisation had not reached its present state, the art of the executioner was indispensable when governments wished to secure blind obedience from their subjects.

The most important information which excavations supply on the last thirty years of Carthage is undoubtedly the radical religious reform which accompanied the political revolution. As already mentioned, roughly two superimposed levels can be distinguished at the *tophet* of Salammbo. The older is characterised by massive sandstone cippi, decorated in Egyptian style; the more recent by limestone steles shaped like obelisks. Stratigraphy establishes the date at which one succeeded the other at about the middle of the fifth century, that is to say, corresponding to the fall of the Magonids. But this change in the equipment of worship indicates not only an evolution of ritual. The rare inscriptions engraved on the cippi invoke a single god, simply called "Ba'al". The thousands of dedications engraved on the steles give first place to the Lady Tanit, "the face of Ba'al", and only second to the Lord Ba'al Hammon. This reversal of precedence is peculiar to Carthage. It is not found for example at Hadrumetum. Even the epithet "face of Ba'al" reserved for the goddess, seems to indicate that she was originally only considered as the paredros, some sort of reflection of the god. Flaubert imagined Carthaginian religion dominated by a sort of dialectic between the male principle, truculent, cruel and fertile, and the female principle, mysterious, sweet and chaste. This romantic interpretation is not a valid one. But it would certainly seem that around 450 B.C., Punic theological conceptions were completely altered in favour of the Lady, who henceforth became the protectress, the virtual queen of the city.

Religious reformers seldom claim to be innovators. They claim rather that they are rediscovering the true meaning of a tradition, obscured by deviations. It is remarkable that the exaltation of Tanit should be accompanied by the re-emergence of symbols from the very distant past. Almost all the steles show two geometrically accurate signs, designated by their place of honour as emblems of the highest sacred power. One of them, known as "the sign of Tanit", is a triangle surmounted by a bar with raised ends, and a circle. Its silhouette forms a personage with raised arms. Although archæologists have proposed all sorts of ingenious and more or less complicated explanations for it, it probably presents nothing more than the stylisation of an idol, frequently found in second millennium Aegean deposits and notably in Minoan palaces at Crete. The other sign looks like a big-bellied bottle, with a more or less elongated neck. In fact, this is another very old idol, also Aegean, showing the great goddess squatting, with enlarged pelvis and breasts. She is very often posed on an altar with concave sides, itself also characteristic of Cretan and Mycenean monuments found, for example, on the famous relief of the Lion Gate at Mycenae.

The inspiration of Carthaginian religious reform thus seems to be borrowed less from the traditions of Canaan, where the essentials of Phœnician religion originated, than from the world of the Aegean. This is not as surprising as it seems at first sight. Contacts between the Phœnicians and the "Peoples of the Sea" had been close and lasting. Justin tells us that Dido herself had the grand priest of "Juno" brought to Carthage from Cyprus with his Tyrian companions, and a whole troop of sacred slaves. The same influences had been spread by "protocolonisation" along all the coasts of Sicily and southern Italy frequented by Punic boats. Natives, immigrants of Greek or Eastern origin, and even Indo-Europeans from the North, willingly paid homage in these ports to a great all-powerful goddess who shows significant resemblances to Tanit, under all her varied names.

However, the connection between political revolution and religious reform is very much in accordance with the temperament of the Semite peoples. With the Greeks or Romans it was exceptional for political upheaval to involve a change in forms of worship—on the contrary, all the governments applied themselves scrupulously to maintaining them. The evolution of moral ideas was thus completely independent of religion. With the Israelites on the other hand, both the hierarchy of moral values and the organisation of institutions evolve as a function of the conception of God. This would also appear to be the case with Carthage. Here archæology again comes to the aid of the historian by suggesting that the revolution, which aimed both at purifying religion and increasing the authority of the State, was accompanied by a drive for moral and economic austerity.

For a long time explorers of Carthaginian tombs have been surprised at the poverty of those which could be assigned to the fifth and the beginning of the fourth centuries. The first striking fact is the almost complete disappearance of imported objects. Museum collections, so rich in Corinthian or Attic black-figure ceramics, contain practically no examples of the red-figure ceramics which began to appear in Athens shortly before the wars with the Medes. Egyptian objects also disappeared, to be replaced by imitations manufactured locally or in Sardinia. Even Etruria supplied practically nothing any longer. The reasons for this absence are easily understandable. The Carthaginian government, reflecting on the causes of its failures, must have realised the disastrous character of its commercial relations with the Greeks, which seriously cut supplies of raw materials and precious metals and only brought luxury products of no practical utility. It therefore decided to stop them once and for all, and henceforth only imported rare Hellenic products through the agency of its allies in Sicily. This also explains the fact that in this period Carthage did not use money, which had been generally used in Greece and the Persian Empire since the beginning of the sixth century. While trade with the Greeks had been maintained, the Carthaginians had not needed to mint gold, silver or bronze, which they exchanged in the form of ingots against finished products. By continuing to refrain from minting money, they now guaranteed themselves against the contraband which might evade official prohibition, because Greek merchants exacted payment in cash. Trade with the barbarians in the Far West continued to be done by a process of primitive barter, which Herodotus very picturesquely describes: the Phœnicians unpacked their merchandise on the beach and retired. The natives, warned by a smoke signal, then placed the gold they offered in exchange next to it. Individually each party examined the offers of the other, adding to his own until agreement was reached. All possible precautions were thus taken by a tacit and inviolable convention to avoid any clash or fraud.

The economic policy, well advised if unduly severe, required great internal discipline on the part of the Carthaginians, and was scrupulously enforced by the police of the Hundred. The wealthy who directed the government must have set the example by restraining their taste for luxury. Justin speaks of sumptuary laws regulating ostentatious display at wedding festivities. It is very probable that expenditure on funerals was also limited by similar measures to the ones Solon had imposed in Athens a short time before. With rare exceptions, the tombs of the period are poorly endowed with jewels, even those manufactured locally. The economy drive did not even spare the gods. Offerings at the *tophet* and the monuments which accompanied them declined in size and value. Highly paid artists were no longer engaged to carve the abstract symbols which represented the gods.

Moreover, the drive for austerity was very probably supported by a spiritual reaction against Hellenism. According to Justin, the Senate even attempted to forbid the teaching of Greek at the beginning of the fourth century, following an affair of high treason. A stele of Hadrametum, found in the layer of the sanctuary corresponding to this period, for the first time presents a version of Ba'al Hammon which became and remained for several centuries the official image of the god. The inspiration is entirely Oriental. Ba'al is seated on a throne decorated with a sphinx, clad in a long robe and wearing a tiara on his head (replaced elsewhere by a crown of feathers) of Mesopotamian origin. Armed with a spear or an axe, he raises his right hand in benediction. The monument very closely resembles a contemporary relief discovered at Tripoli in Syria, showing Astarte on her throne in front of a worshipper. The theme was therefore borrowed from Asia, without Hellenic contamination. This nationalist reaction succeeded in saving Phœnician civilisation in Africa at the very time it disappeared from Asia. There is a striking contrast between Carthaginian monuments of this period, such as those just described, and the sarcophagi sculptured after 450 B.C. by Greek artists of the Attic School for the Kings of Sidon. Even the names of these princes from that time onwards are purely Hellenic. Furthermore, the national language was abandoned in Libya, to be replaced by Greek or Aramaic, used by the Persian administration. It is remarkable that precisely at this period Phœnician inscriptions multiplied at Carthage.

Perhaps the school of traditionalist scribes, no longer finding pupils in their own country, emigrated to Africa and spread a culture there which, before that time, had been fairly circumscribed. But there is no doubt that artists' studios in Carthage, which were already very mediocre, suffered greatly from the neglect to which they were condemned. In the preceding century, they had learned some formulae from the Greeks of Sicily. Knowing absolutely nothing of the revolution which had given birth to classicism, they continued to reproduce them mechanically. Therefore, works are found at Carthage which were being sculptured right up to the very destruction of the city, according to conventions abandoned at Greece several centuries earlier. A funeral statue at the necropolis of Santa Monica from the third century still shows the almond-shaped eyes and clean shaven face of the sixth-century Athenian *Kouroi*—and, furthermore, retains none of the vigour and freshness of the old masters. When relations with the Hellenic world were renewed, the split had been so deep that the genius of the artists was completely immunised against it. The Greeks could then instal themselves alongside the traditionalist studios, where the artists were so deeply sunk in their routine that they understood nothing of an aesthetic which had become as foreign to them as that of Matisse and Picasso might today be to the carvers of the statues at Saint Sulpice.

These results of their policy certainly escaped the senators and the *rabs* who presided over the Carthaginian "pentarchies". Graver problems demanded their attention. They had to find substitutes for the merchandise which no longer came to their ports because of the stoppage of trade. They had to repair the losses inflicted by Gelon on the Magonids, and also to accumulate in treasuries, shops and arsenals reserves needed to face the ultimate Greek assault. The first necessity was to keep alive. Because boats no longer brought corn and oil, these had to be produced locally, utilising a hinterland which had till then been neglected. The Libyans had to be forced to abandon primitive pastoral economy and be turned into farmers. S. Gsell has established that the conquest of the interior of Tunisia and the development of agriculture were the great work of the Carthaginians in the fifth century. Until then the Libyans had remained masters even of the outskirts of the town, which had to pay a tribute to them. It has already been seen how they profited from the defeat of Himera to tighten their grip. The last of the Magonids were most anxious to efface this shame. In a relatively short time they succeeded in subduing a territory the limits of which are not known exactly but which must have covered a good part of Tunisia. In any case, it included the peninsula of Cape Bon, the plains of the Lower Medjerda and the hills of the Sahel, that is to say, the most fertile parts of present-day Tunisia. No time was lost in developing them. At the beginning of the fourth century, the soldiers of Agathocles, marching towards Carthage after landing at the point of Cape Bon, were amazed at the fertility of the countryside, full of vines and olives and fruit trees. In fact, this region was particularly favourable for orchards while the plains of the interior were better suited to cereals. Expert agricultural-ists determined the most suitable processes to utilise the soil—certainly more fertile than it is today—and to compensate for the irregularity of the rainfall. One of them, Mago, was considered by the Greeks and Romans to be a pastmaster at this science and his works were translated into Latin.

The subjugation of the interior naturally reinforced the authority of Carthage over the Phoenician ports bordering the coasts. More-over, it is probable that new colonists were sent to most of them, and transformed the mediocre trading stations which hitherto had been sufficient for the requirements of commerce, into townships. The most ancient deposits of the *tophet* of Hadrumetum only go back to the sixth century and recent English excavations in the towns of Tripolitania have discovered nothing before the fifth century. In actuality, these cities were neither docile nor faithful to the metropolis in after years. They were jealous of it and it also treated them rather badly. In general, it cannot be said that Carthage was able to inspire love in its subjects. There is little information on the conditions of the Libyans, though it would seem that they must have been poor, for they seized every opportunity to revolt. However, the Punic civilisa-tion held some attractions for them. Rural necropolises have been excavated, particularly in Cape Bon, where the dead were buried according to Berber rites, the corpse squatting and painted red, but accompanied by Punic tomb furniture. The Greeks acquired the habit of designating this population, which soon adopted a large part of the language, religion and customs of its masters, by the name of Libyo-Phoenician.

The conquest of the mainland provinces did not make the Cartha-ginians neglect the colonial empire. On the contrary, they seem to have tried to renew bonds with the most distant countries, loosened by the decline of trade with Tarshish. It is generally agreed that the most famous of the great Punic explorations actually took place in the fifth century. In the north Hamilco advanced along the Spanish and Gallic coast at least as far as Finisterre. He visited the Island of Ushant, which served as a relay station for tin from Cornwall. But the most daring and important enterprises were directed towards the south, along the African coasts. According to Herodotus, the Pharaoh Nechao (609-594 B.C.), subsidised a Phoenician expedition which succeeded in circumnavigating Africa in three years. Doubt has been thrown on this exploit, which remained unique. It might however have been repeated around 470 B.C., if the Persian, Sataspes, had had more strength of character. This cousin of King Xerxes, condemned to death for violating the daughter of another nobleman, was reprieved on condition he made a tour of Africa. He sailed on an Egyptian ship, through the Pillars of Hercules and far on to the south until he came to a country inhabited by pygmies clad in palm leaves, who fled at his approach. He then made the mistake of losing heart and returning to the king who, keeping strictly to the custom of the country, had him impaled.

It may be said that the Carthaginians neither initiated nor directed these two expeditions which nevertheless concerned their own realm, but certainly neither of them could have been carried out without their assistance. This demonstrates very well that until the beginning of the fifth century the new Tyre still remained simply an advance post of the eastern empires. On the other hand, the expedition of "King" Hanno—probably one of the last of the Magonids—which undoubtedly took place about 450 B.C., seems to have been solely a Punic enterprise. It was animated by a double wish to impose the hegemony of Carthage on the extreme western Phoenician establishments and to monopolise their resources to her own advantage. A Greek translation has been preserved of an account of it, which was engraved in the Temple of Ba'al Hammon at Carthage. This fascinating text unfortunately poses innumerable problems which specialists are still discussing. Furthermore, Carcopino has shown that the Greek adapter, no doubt deliberately misled by the Carthaginians, has only given a truncated version; details of distances and changes of direction are omitted, rendering it useless to the sailor seeking nautical information. Leaving with a numerous fleet, Hanno began by visiting and reinforcing the towns founded earlier by Carthage on the eastern coast of Morocco. The destination of this first stage was the Island of Cerne, undoubtedly Hern, opposite the Rio de Oro. Hanno used it as a base for several expeditions southwards. These led him first to a great lake overhung by high mountains, where the savage inhabitants drove him away with stones, and then to a river full of hippopotami. On a second voyage, after skirting wooded mountains and crossing a large gulf where great fires rose at night on every bank, they arrived at another bay which the interpreters call "Horn of the West". "In this gulf there was a large island and in the island a lagoon which enclosed another island. Disembarking there, in the daytime we only saw a forest. But at night many fires appeared and we heard the sounds of a flute, the clash of cymbals and tambourines, and a very loud noise. Fear seized us and the soothsayers ordered us to leave the island." The Carthaginians then came to a burning land, full of perfumes, and crossed by flaming streams which plunged into the sea. These out-flows of lava descended from a volcano named the Chariot of the Gods. Further on, they arrived at another island, peopled by gorillas. They captured three females and brought the skins back to Carthage. Lack of provisions finally forced them to return. Modern exegetists have used a great deal of ingenuity in identifying the places described by Hanno. However, it would be very difficult indeed to do this successfully. The most likely hypothesis recognises the volcano "The Chariot of the Gods" as Mount Cameroon, in which case the voyage would have ended in the Gulf of Guinea.

These are the most remarkable episodes of a voyage that is some-times reminiscent of the adventures of Captain Cook, sometimes of Sinbad the Sailor.

This subject poses the problem of the possibilities open to the Carthaginian navy. It has again been contested recently whether the Carthaginians could have gone beyond Cape Juby to the north of Rio de Oro. Prevailing winds would have prevented ancient sailing boats advancing further south, while rowing boats would not have been able to venture along the coast of the Sahara Desert without condemning their galley rowers to perishing of thirst.

There are equally obvious arguments against these sceptics. If the immense rivers, full of crocodiles and hippopotami, described by Hanno, flowed in the Moroccan Sahara, if thick forests grew there and if negroes and particularly pygmies lived there, the climate must have been entirely different from today. In that case, arguments cannot be based on the present state of wind and water.

It is particularly imprudent to try to verify the data of the texts on the basis of our present very limited knowledge of ancient technique. Some thirty years ago, Commandant Lefèvre des Noettes demon-strated the frailty of the means of transport used by ancient peoples: teams of animals, for instance, would have been paralysed by the type of collar that was used, which would have strangled the beasts, and shoeing was unknown. The possibility of using boats—and this is the relevant point in the present case—would have been restricted, he said, by their necessarily haphazard steering, as the rudder at the stern-post did not appear until the twelfth century.

Since then, these theories have for the most part been very rightly questioned. Expert sailors have disputed the value of the rudder at the stern-post. But until now, as far as we know, Madame M. Hours has been the only one to recognise that this famous device very frequently and clearly figures on Punic steles. Could the knowledge of the rudder at the stern-post perhaps have been the secret which assured the fortunes of Carthage? We do not think so. Firstly, the facility with which the Romans, who had so little natural bent for the sea, managed to deal with the Punic navy makes it difficult to believe that the latter possessed vastly superior technique. And secondly, because reproductions of these rudders on the steles of the *tophet*, to which foreigners were allowed access, proves that their manufacture was not a state secret.

It is a pity that the engravings and paintings of boats surviving from Punic art are so poor. The shapeless designs only produce one piece of really fundamental information: the use of the rudder at the stern-post. On the other hand, a great deal of information exists on mosaics regarding the boats of Roman Africa. But these were constructed in the old Phoenician cities, the two Hippos, the ports of Byzacium, and the Emporia in Tripolitania. At Carthage, Scipio seized the completely equipped arsenal and immediately took on the two thousand men who had been working there. The secrets of the Punic shipbuilders could therefore not have escaped Rome, and the rudder at the stern-post must have been known to all the Mediterranean navies, although it was not used a great deal, 1,500 years earlier than Lefèvre des Noettes had thought.

The importance of the absence of Punic discoveries south of Mogador must also not be exaggerated. Phoenician objects are also absent from the Atlantic coasts of France and very rare in Great Britain. The secrets of Mogador were only revealed in 1950 and P. Cintas, who directed excavations, is firmly convinced of the existence of Punic sites further south, as far as the island of Hern—where he agrees with Carcopino in locating Cerne.

It can be guessed that it was not mere curiosity which impelled the Carthaginians to advance so far in the face of innumerable dangers. In the ancient world, which was fairly poor in gold mines, the placer deposits at Senegal were one of the principal sources of the precious metal. The text of Herodotus, cited above, proves that the Carthaginians were supplied from this source. So great was the attraction which this Eldorado exercised on them that they did not hesitate to approach it by another and even more perilous route than the ocean. The Sahara, as has been mentioned, did not form an absolutely insuperable barrier. If the goodwill of the Garamantes, the predecessors and possible ancestors of the Tuaregs was assured, it was possible to reach the Sudan with horses harnessed to light chariots, carrying water-skins attached beneath their bellies. Athenaeus recalls a certain Mago who is claimed to have crossed the desert three times—without drinking anything.

At first sight it is paradoxical that the fifth and fourth century Carthaginians should have inflicted so much hardship on themselves to ensure supplies of rare and precious articles from distant markets just at the time when they had practically renounced trading with the Greeks, or when these latter were preventing them from communicating with the Orient. They were certainly not driven by a taste for luxury and ostentation, because the poverty of their necropolises and sanctuaries bears witness to an austerity which borders on avarice. In actuality, the Carthaginians' "lust for gold" can be explained by the fear in which Carthage lived and by the necessity of maintaining a military force capable of discouraging the greed of the Greeks, and of one day revenging Himera. Already in the sixth century the Magonids had widely employed mercenaries for their wars with Sicily. Possibly, like other "tyrants", they had more confidence in these foreigners than in their compatriots. However, the oligarchy did not change this policy. It was undoubtedly guided by the need to use as economically as possible the civic body of Phoenician origin, which it was becoming difficult to reinforce by immigration. When the African territorial empire was constituted, Carthage sought to raise colonial troops there. But the Libyans, who were brave but at a low stage of development, could supply scarcely anything but auxiliaries whose fidelity was not always above suspicion. In the tactics of the period, the most important elements of the armies were constituted by the phalanx of Hoplites, heavily-armed infantrymen, who were accustomed to strict discipline. Even the Greeks tended to have greater and greater recourse to professionals, who were naturally better trained than civilian soldiers. The condottieri who collected them together were not guided by any high ideals. From the end of the fourth century, some Greek chiefs did not hesitate to offer their bands for service to Carthage against their fellow countrymen.

The economy of Carthage in the fifth century and at the beginning of the fourth was therefore dominated by the same national and religious impetus which inspired the reform of its institutions. It is completely misguided to see it as a form of mercantilism, a desire for hegemony based on commercial and industrial superiority. In these spheres, Carthage remained vastly inferior to the Greeks. Its ideas on the employment of the metallic reserves which its exploitation of the West put at its disposal, were just as simple as those of the King of Persia. They were confined to the constitution of a war-chest utilised exclusively for political ends: the payment of troops, subsidies to allies or the corruption of political opponents. The efficiency of these proceedings is corroborated elsewhere by the Greeks themselves. In a discourse which Thucydides attributes to him, the Syracusan orator Hermocrates informs us that in 427 B.C., the Carthaginians had considerable wealth in gold and silver at their disposal, and were advising his compatriots to call on them to help resist the Athenian attack. The Punic oligarchy did not think of profiting by the great conflict which divided the Hellenic world to mount a counter-attack, perhaps because it did not yet feel assured of its African bases or because it hoped that its enemies would destroy themselves. This hope was crushed because although Athens was worsted in the war, Syracuse emerged stronger than ever, and worked unceasingly to extend its hegemony to the whole island. Carthage then decided to put into motion the strength it had been accumulating over more than half a century. Undoubtedly a sort of sacred union made it forget political divisions: supreme command was entrusted to a Magonid, Hannibal, the grandson of Hamilcar, the conquered leader at Himera.

The first expedition (409 B.C.) met with complete success. Hannibal destroyed Selinus and Himera and sacrificed three thousand prisoners to the spirits of his ancestors. Three years later came the turn of Agrigentum and Gela. All Greek Sicily was threatened with horrible destruction as the Carthaginians and their wild auxiliaries vied with each other in cruelty. Their relentlessness revealed an inexpiable racial hatred, again aggravated by religious fanaticism. The visitor to Selinunte and Girgenti can still judge the atrocity and efficiency of the destruction. In the ruins of the temples only humble hovels were rebuilt.

Dionysius of Syracuse was the saviour of western Hellenism. In 397 B.C., the old Phœnician colony of Motya, which was as old as Carthage, met the same fate as Selinus. The war continued for almost forty years with alternating Greek successes and reverses. When it ended, Carthage only retained the old country of Elymi to the west of Selinus.

In the following generation the Carthaginians found themselves threatened with a destruction as radical as that with which they had threatened the Greeks. A new Syracusan tyrant, Agathocles, landed on the point of Cape Bon in 324 B.C., devastated the regions which

supplied Carthage with essential provisions and was the first to blockade the town itself. This enterprise was too audacious and ended in
disaster. But the Carthaginians had definitely lost the upper hand in
Sicily and Agathocles had shown the path which Regulus and Scipio
would later follow.

Thus, the great Punic revolution ended in setback. Carthage felt
it had been abandoned by the gods in whom it had put all its hope.
When it was besieged by Agathocles, the inhabitants organised a
monstrous *auto-da-fé* of all noble children who had been allowed to
escape the "Moloch" by substitution now considered fraudulent. But
already in 396 B.C., scruples of another kind had led to the establishment of a sanctuary on the hill of Bordj Djedid, dedicated to the two
goddesses of Syracuse, Demeter and Koré, who had avenged the
pillaging of one of their temples in Sicily by plague. The absolute
intransigence by which the Punic oligarchy had hoped to hold its own
against Hellenism was becoming exhausted. Its political and social
stability were being challenged; its own military chiefs again began
to fight against it. When peace was concluded with Dionysius, the old
army leader, Hanno the Great, prepared to assassinate the whole
Senate at one blow during his daughter's wedding celebrations. He
perished under atrocious torture. But what is perhaps more serious is
that he had been supported by an army of freed slaves and that he had
called in the Moors: the conquest of the hinterland states and the
rigorous exploitation imposed on the great empires had given birth
to a poor and savage proletariat whom the unruly natives were ready
to support. This peril, in conjunction with the hostility of the foreign
powers, resulted in the final ruin of Carthage.

However, it would be unjust to condemn the revival of the fifth
century absolutely. It is undoubtedly regrettable that Carthage could
only assert itself by self-denial and not by creating a civilisation
capable of competing with Hellenism. Its reaction bears some resemblance to that of Sparta which also, about the beginning of the
sixth century, deliberately broke the course of its evolution, renounced
the charms of liberalism and even mutilated its economy to preserve
political power in the hands of a closed caste as long as possible. The
similarity which Aristotle noted between the institutions of the two
cities does not appear so superficial. In the case of Carthage, however,
it is necessary to take into account a religious psychology, of which
the manifestations cannot be separated from political facts, and which
differs profoundly from anything found in Greece. But, just as Sparta
is definitively fixed in history as the city of Lycurgus, that is to say,
undoubtedly that of Chilo, the essential features which Carthage has

preserved are those which the crisis of the fifth century imposed on it. A Greek rhetor of the imperial period, Dio of Prusia, surnamed Chrysostom, fairly justly defined the essential of this reform, the initiative of which he attributes to the Magonid, Hanno: "He transformed the Carthaginians, Tyrians as they were, into Libyans. Thanks to him, they inhabited Libya instead of Phœnicia, acquired a great deal of wealth, numerous markets, ports and triremes, and were supreme far and wide, over land and sea." Granted that the Carthaginians then ceased to consider themselves simply as a colony of Tyre, and understood the necessity of organising in Libya a state capable of independent existence and of transplanting and developing in it a Phœnician civilisation. Their hope was obviously to eliminate Hellenism and to make the whole western basin of the Mediterranean the exclusive realm of this culture, jeopardised in its place of origin. If they were not able to succeed in this, they did at least succeed in ensuring for it in Africa a vitality which managed to resist for almost a millennium the seductions of Hellenism, even when supported by the imperial power of Rome.

V

HELLENISTIC CARTHAGE

AT the beginning of the fourth century it might have been expected that after a hundred years of almost uninterrupted war against the Greeks of Sicily during which defeats had on the whole outnumbered victories, Carthage would be weakened and less likely than ever to accept the civilisation of its enemies. On the contrary, however, the much greater wealth of the tombs of this period shows that the standard of living had risen. Archaeologists have also noted the reappearance in quantity of the products of Hellenic art and industry which had been almost entirely banned since the beginning of the fifth century. This new paradox is actually explained firstly by the circumstances of the war. Apart from Agathocles' expedition, it had taken place in Sicily. The visitor to Selinus and Agrigentum can still appreciate the atrocity of the struggle which laid waste the whole southern part of the island, previously the scene of vigorous life. As a result of the systematic use of mercenaries, this war scarcely raised any but economic problems for the Carthaginian government, for which the exploitation of the states of the hinterland and the ports of the western Mediterranean supplied ample resources.

Better still, the war itself was certainly remunerative. The pillaging of all the great Sicilian cities, only Syracuse excepted, had accumulated a pile of riches in Punic treasuries and temples which Scipio still found there a century and a half later. On the other hand, Dionysius, Timoleon and Agathocles never won victories that were decisive enough to claim the payment of a substantial war indemnity. By making use of this booty, the Carthaginians once again became accustomed to using the advantages of Hellenic civilisation. They were already prepared for this by their contacts with prisoners, who had been reduced to slavery. These included artisans and cultured men, deserters and mercenaries recruited in Greece, whose services the Republic increasingly sought and who were not necessarily old troopers. As early as 396 B.C., a Greek colony is known to have lived peaceably at Carthage, despite the fact that the latter was then engaged in a particularly bitter phase of its battle against Syracuse. The priests of Demeter who had the status of official personages were

[46] Mosaic from Thuburbo Majus showing negro camel-drivers. It is one of the pieces of evidence which help to solve the enigma of the camel in North Africa. It was certainly introduced before the first century B.C. but only played an important role after the third century A.D. Furthermore, the camel is only useful in the Saharan or Pre-Saharan area, whereas nearly all our documents refer to the Tell.

[47] Scylla, the guardian of the straits of Sicily. The Carthaginians and the Etruscans shared with the Greeks the fear of this monster and of many other fantastic sea creatures (note the hippocampus in the next illustration). Terra cotta medallion found at Kerkouane (Cape Bon). About 200 B.C.

[48] Bow of a Punic galley—the reverse side of a coin struck by Hasdrubal in Spain (228-221 B.C.). The obverse side is shown in Ill. 28.

[49 and 50] Central Africa as seen by the Ancient peoples. Mosaics from the second century A.D. discovered at Chebba and Hadrumetum show the countryside of the Upper Nile according to Egyptian prototypes of the Alexandrian period. It is known that explorers reached Bahr el Gahazal. The countryside, described according to their accounts, is similar to that described by Hanno. Notice particularly the Pygmies fighting crocodiles and hippopotamuses. The climate and fauna of equatorial Africa were therefore the same as at present.

[50]

[51] Alexandrian askos originating from a Punic tomb at Cape Bon.

[52] Lamp discovered in a tomb at Cape Bon: divine head and frog. (*Photo Bouchoucha*).

ustrations 52 to 55 illustrate Carthaginian trade with the Hellenistic states.

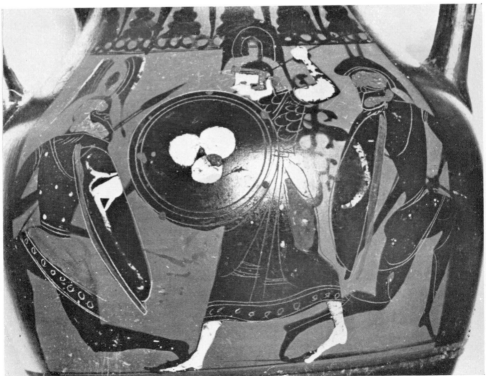

[53] Decoration of a Greek vase from Italy, discovered in a Punic tomb at Cape Bon.

[54] Ivory plaque representing Aphrodite carried on a swan.

[55] Bathroom in a house in a small Punic town at the point of Cape Bon.

[56] Handle of a bronze wine-vase, representing the head of Silenus.

chosen from among them, which proves that they were distinguished and respected. The Sicilian allies of the Carthaginians, notably the Elymi, were on their part quietly converted to Greek civilisation. This can be seen from the great Doric temple at Segesta, their principal town, and by the money they minted. Even Palermo, the Phœnician capital in Sicily, is only known by its Greek name and its coinage is completely Hellenic.

More basic reasons moreover forced Carthage to put an end to its isolation. The wars of the fifth century had assured the Greeks control of the eastern Mediterranean. Those of the fourth had made them masters of the whole civilised world. The Carthaginians learned with consternation in 332 B.C. that Alexander was besieging their metropolis of Tyre. They were still united to it by filial affection, expressed by sending a sacred tribute to Melqart each year. The ambassadors entrusted with this pious mission, were present during the atrocious seven-month siege and were able to judge the danger of opposing the conqueror by the fate of their compatriots, who were pitilessly condemned to death or slavery. Alexander spared the lives of the delegates, but informed them that he would soon attack their native land. Several diplomatic and spying missions only confirmed to the Punic government that the king persevered in his intentions. At his death, a memorandum was found in which he had drafted the outlines for a combined naval and land expedition westwards. Carthage would have been its primary target.

If the Greco-Macedonian empire had remained united, the Phœnicians in Africa would probably not have been able to escape expropriation. Its break-up saved them. Preoccupied with their struggles, the Diadochi and their successors could not think of new conquests. Only Pyrrhus of Epirus thought for a moment of becoming the Alexander of the West but neither his forces nor his talents measured up to those of his model. He only succeeded in occupying the Punic province of Sicily for a very short period (278–276 B.C.).

At this time the East experienced a period of calm. Conquest by Alexander and then his death, had brought about fifty years of desperate and confused fighting from which great dynasties finally emerged: the Antigonids in Macedonia, the Seleucids of Asia, and the Ptolemies of Egypt. Only the most remarkable of the new kings, Ptolemy, son of Lagos, conceived and almost realised a hegemony, which did not depend on military force but on economic and naval superiority. He joined Coele-Syria, that is to say Palestine and Phœnicia, and Cyrenaica to Egypt, a country where the immense natural resources were methodically exploited, rendering it unequalled in the East. Deliberately breaking the economic unity of the Greco-Macedonian world, he imposed Phœnician measures and money on his whole empire. There is no doubt that the Phœnicians understood the advantages to be derived from this situation. Their heavily ravaged towns found security and prosperity once more. Carthage had everything to gain and associated itself freely with this community which united all the nations with whom its traditions and interests already linked it. And the Ptolemies had every advantage on their side in bringing the resources of the Far West to Alexandria by way of Carthage, in addition to those of the Far East which the mastery of the Red Sea procured them.

In agreeing to enter into this economic unity, Carthage resumed its commercial place in the Greek world. Only then did the Punic merchant become a familiar figure in all Mediterranean ports. Inscriptions bear witness to his presence at Athens and Delos. Although Thebes was not a great trading centre, it elected a sort of consul charged with guarding its interests at Carthage. Humorous authors amused their public with their picture of the Semite merchant, in a long, flowing robe and with an incomprehensible language and barbarous superstitions. Plautus, transposing a Greek play, thus puts on the stage a certain Hanno who lands at Calydon in Aetolia, where he is to stay. Carthaginian tourists carved their names on the back of a Sphinx, in the Serapion at Memphis.

In these circumstances it is not surprising that a large quantity of Greek objects exist in third and second century Carthaginian necropolises. Some of them come directly from Alexandria, as for example a beautiful *askos* (a flat vase with a wide, short spout) decorated with the fore-part of a bull, or a small perfume vase, shaped like a negrillo. Greek lamps of Attic or Rhodian design successfully competed with the old bowls with their curled edges. Some are veritable works of art. One particularly, found in a tomb at Cape Bon, has a lid in the shape of a human head, while the base represents a frog. The bearded head, with black enamel eyes inlaid with gold, is of striking nobility and undoubtedly represents a god. It is Egyptian symbolism which explains the strange association of the human face and the batrachian. The frog appeared on the banks of the Nile, where thousands of tadpoles hatch out with the floods in the fertile mud, the very symbol of renascent life, of human resurrection after death. The object was therefore undoubtedly manufactured at Alexandria, where many frog-shaped lamps were still being made several centuries later.

Their entrance into Egyptian commerce obliged the Carthaginians to adopt money. As early as the end of the fifth century, they had resigned themselves to minting it in Sicily, but only for use by their mercenaries who would not accept payment in kind. The coins minted there had the same weight as those of the Greeks of the island —that is to say they conformed to the Attic standard. On the other hand, the money issued at Carthage itself after the fourth century, was cut to the Phœnician standard, as was the Egyptian. There is no doubt therefore that this reform, which upset the Punic commercial system, was due to Alexandrian influence. Under the guidance of Egyptian financiers, the most knowledgable of the ancient world, the Carthaginians made up at least a part of the arrears of over two centuries caused by the conservatism of their aristocracy. Undoubtedly, they did not succeed in organising in their own country such a perfect institution as the famous royal bank which centralised the revenues of Egypt, and served as an instrument of high politics. But they availed themselves of its good offices, when they could. It is known that during the first Punic War they solicited a loan of two thousand talents, which was however refused.

There was also active trade with the colonies of Magna Graecia. They produced painted vases, less elegant than those of Athens, which are found in quite large numbers in the Punic tombs of the period, together with terra cotta, bronze and ivory statuettes of the same origin. The number of Greeks settled at Carthage naturally grew in proportion to this trade. The epitaph of a Cyrenian, Pamphila, the daughter of Agesandros and consequently a subject of the Ptolemies, has been exhumed near the public baths of Antoninus. She must have followed her father or her husband to the Punic capital. Another Greek, Euklea, dedicated an ex-voto to Tanit and Ba'al Hammon. The Punic religion therefore had a certain attraction for the immigrants, despite the horror of its rites. But above all, it was the Carthaginians who borrowed from their guests. They learned from them how to construct more comfortable houses, decorated to the taste of the day. In the last few years excavations have revealed the houses of a village of fishermen and purple dyers situated at the point of Cape Bon, at a place called Kerkouane, destroyed at the same time as Carthage. One of them possessed a perfectly fitted bathroom, exactly the same as those found in Greece, at Corinth for example. There is a "shoe" type bath-tub, in which the bather sat on a bench next to a little basin undoubtedly for washing his face and hands. The floors were covered with a sort of mosaic of cement encrusted with small cubes of marble. This style spread simultaneously through the whole western Mediterranean. The ruins of a whole district of Carthage dating from this period still exist beneath the Roman constructions, in the southern part of the plateau of the hill of Byrsa. The houses were decorated with elegant pillars of stuccoed sandstone bearing Ionic capitals, and were served by drains.

An ingenious design, traced on the wall of a tomb, in a necropolis at Cape Bon, represents an old fortified town. Seventeen constructions of great height rise in the centre of a turretted surrounding wall. They had extensive ground floors, a sort of gallery or loggia above, and a capping formed of three or four domes or rounded turrets, and thus very much resembled country houses represented on African mosaics of the imperial period. It can thus be conjectured that the type of towered house in general use in the Hellenic world and notably in Egypt, was adopted at Carthage, not only in the country, but also in the towns. Hannibal possessed one of these "towers" in Byzacium, the present-day Sahel. At Carthage itself, three roads leading from the public square to the acropolis of Byrsa were lined with six-storeyed houses. As for the temples, the Egyptian style was a thing of the past. Their appearance can be gathered from a miniature chapel discovered at Thuburbo Majus, which reproduces a temple to Demeter. Two Ionic colonettes, identical with those at Carthage, support an entablature, overloaded—in defiance of all the rules of classical aesthetics—with an accumulation of ornaments borrowed from the Hellenic repertoire: denticles, ovolos and spearheads, beading and whirligigs. Moreover the artists made use of motifs belonging to their own tradition at the same time, such as the Egyptian groove or capitals decorated with the bust of the goddess Hathor. Alexandrian taste also appreciated this mixture of orientalism and Hellenism but it mixed the elements with more moderation.

Under Hellenic influence, a true art then seemed about to be born at Carthage for the first time. The greatest successes were realised by engravings on metal or stone. For two centuries, strangely-shaped blades had been placed in tombs, one side finished with a curved edge, the other carved in the shape of a swan's neck. They resemble the razors used by the ancient Egyptians and still retained till quite recently by some negro tribes of the African interior. From the fourth century onwards, the flat part was generally decorated with an engraving, first representing Egyptian divinities—such as Isis, Horus, and Anubis—and then Greek gods, assimilated, as will be seen, to the Punic gods—Hercules and Hermes. The most recently discovered blade, at Utica, shows Hercules strangling the bull of Crete on one side and on the other, the monster Scylla, the terror of the Straits of Sicily. This legend may possibly have been told the Greeks by the Phœnicians. The technique is related to that of the Etruscan mirrors,

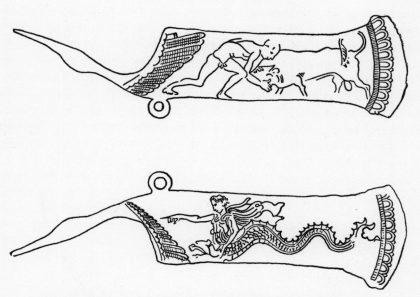

Punic razor with Hellenistic decoration originating
from Utica: Heracles throttling the bull of Crete; the
monster Scylla.

but does not attain their quality. However, the few metallic mirrors
discovered at Carthage are bare of all ornament. Greek influence also
transformed the subjects engraved on the flat part of the seals, the
backs of which continued to be cut in the form of scarabs. Some, such
as a ring at Utica with an image of Pegasus, rise to the heights of
masterpieces. The glassmakers, who had been famous for a long time,
gave free play to their imagination, producing amusing amulets in
coloured paste, minute masks to replace the large terra cotta ones
and exercising the same prophylactic powers. Some represent men
with curled blue hair and beards, yellow skin and enormous eyes in
white enamel, others, women with pallid complexions, like the female
masks in Greek comedy. Tiny jars in marbled glass were sold throughout the western Mediterranean. Manufacturers of purple dye also
worked for export. Thousands of broken murex shells accumulated on
the beach by which the village of Kerkouane stands. It was the de-
caying flesh of the murex which produced the royal dye. As enormous
quantities of murex were needed to yield a small quantity of purple,
all the trading stations spaced out along the coasts as far as the extremities of Morocco collected the precious crustaceans. Their debris

is one of the most certain indications of a Punic settlement. Furthermore, plants from the Moroccan coast provided a less expensive
substitute, which the Carthaginians also used when necessary. Finally,
from the mass of steles of the *tophet* decorated only with the usual
symbols of abstract Punic theology, a few pieces are outstanding,
line-engraved with a vigour and sureness of touch which reveal the
hand of a master. One of the most beautiful is in the Lavigerie
Museum, and portrays the bust of a young man in a chlamys,

Punic razor in style imitated from Egypt.

undoubtedly Hermes, whose pathetic expression is reminiscent of Scopas. This success was an exception. Next to it, another bust of Hermes, with a petasus on his head, is disappointing because of its lack of expression and vigour, and remains very inferior to the "Priest with Child" in pure Phœnician tradition. Another stele is only engraved with a picture of a large metal vase, whose elegant curves, the acanthus leaves which decorate the belly and the foot, fluted like a column, could only have originated in a Greek workshop. Elsewhere, a delicate fleuron is inserted between the inscription and the symbol of the inverted crescent moon on the disc, marrying the stylised form of the lotus and acanthus. The fantasies of Alexandrian artists, combining branches of foliage and animated figures, are adopted at Carthage earlier than Rome. Terra cotta plaques decorating divine thrones already showed elegant Victories, bearing helmets and trophies, which reappeared on the stuccos of the Farnesine a hundred years later. The monster, Scylla, had already changed into one of the hybrid beings, half-human, half-vegetable, which later irritated the down-to-earth common-sense of Vitruvius.

Alexandrian influence undoubtedly explains one of the most interesting problems of Punic archaeology. From the fourth century pits were cut in the limestone hill of Santa Monica which overlooks the town to the north. These were sometimes sixty feet deep, and led to funeral caves for the members of the Carthaginian aristocracy. The most wealthy reposed in marble sarcophagi, four of which have statues on their lids. Two represent women: one enveloped in a long cloak covering her head, which she thrusts aside with her right hand, exactly reproduces a fourth-century Greek type. The other wears a more fantastic costume than any with which Flaubert chose to clothe *Salammbô*: a costume representing the skin of an immense dove, of which the head served as a helmet and the crossed wings formed a robe. This is certainly a divine costume of Egyptian origin. It could not have been, as is generally believed, the sacerdotal garment of the priestess, whose skeleton—that of an old and ugly woman, possibly of negroid type—lies in the tunnel. Moreover, it is not certain that the epitaph to the priestess, Arishat, found next to it, belongs to the tomb. It was more likely to have been the supernatural robe of Tanit, who watched over the last sleep of her adherent. The two statues of men, bearded, their hands raised in a gesture of benediction rather than prayer, wear a long tunic covered by a sort of cloak. A very similar sarcophagus shelters the body of an Etruscan in the necropolis of Tarquinia. It is also thought in some quarters that the sarcophagi at Carthage were imported from Italy. Others, in view of the Aegean origin of the marble, think them to be Greek work. This shows little appreciation of the eminently Punic character of the statues: the feminine costume formed from the skin of a bird is also worn by the terra cotta statue of a goddess with the head of a lion, found at Thinissut, in Cape Bon, in the ruins of a temple to Tanit. The masculine costume—the long tunic decorated with a cloak across the shoulder—is found again on steles, statuettes, and on an engraved funeral casket. The gesture of the raised hand, with the palm open, had such important symbolic value that a hand thus represented was sufficient to evoke the divinity on the fronton of many steles. There is therefore no doubt whatsoever that the sarcophagi were sculptured at Carthage itself, undoubtedly by immigrant Greek sculptors. Moreover, the name of one of these artists who must have lived in the Punic capital during the last years of its existence has been preserved. He was Boethos, the Carthaginian, the namesake, by some strange chance, of a famous bronze-founder originally from Chalcedon. His masterpiece, "The Contest" or "Spirit of the Palaestra", was found in the open sea off Mahdia, on the east coast of Tunisia. It had been lost there in a shipwreck at the beginning of the first century B.C.

It has already been stated that these Greek sculptors only worked for the élite. The Carthaginian masses continued to patronise native workshops, which were still carving shapeless images showing degenerate forms of the processes of Greek antiquity, transmitted two centuries earlier through the agency of Carthage and Etruria. However, these crude works have a certain austere nobility, but even this is no longer found in a statue of Tanit in stuccoed sandstone, disjointed fragments of which are preserved at the Lavigerie Museum. The veiled goddess is seated on a throne guarded by sphinxes. A little hollowed niche on the lower side of the seat contains another image of a woman holding a child on her knees, undoubtedly Demeter Kourotrophos. The monument is valuable from the point of view of religious history, but the lack of vigour of the treatment is worthy of the worst marble-mason in a provincial Italian cemetery. Often, moreover, for the sake of economy, temples were only decorated with terra cotta statues. This form of art, abandoned by the Greeks since the fifth century, was also practised by the Etruscans, who could fashion the material into masterpieces. No African Koroplathos, as far as is known, rose to the level of the masters of Veii. The great terra-cottas discovered at Carthage itself, in a chapel dating from the last days of independence, and particularly at several sanctuaries on Cape Bon, built during the Roman Republic, or at the very beginning of the Empire, emphasise the hopeless vulgarity of the Carthaginians.

The most striking of these is the statue of a goddess with the head of a lion, clad in the same Egyptian costume, imitating the skin of a bird which Tanit wears on the Santa Monica sarcophagus. It is impossible not to be struck by the ferocity of the face, accentuated by its exaggerated eyebrows and the mouth drawn up to expose the fangs. It is a form of the Egyptian Sokhet, undoubtedly copied from a Hellenic-style work of the Ptolemaic period. But the Egyptian lioness, tranquil, noble and, on the whole, benevolent in her power, belonged to a completely different religious conception from that expressed by the barbarous statue of the Punic goddess, thirsting for human blood.

A mother feeding her baby was also worshipped in the same sanctuary, as moving as a village madonna in the clumsiness of her thick-set peasant silhouette. She is Demeter, who during her wanderings humbly agreed to remain as nurse to the little king of Eleusis. Tanit and Demeter, the savage virgin and the sad, good mother, would seem to form a strange couple. But the Homeric hymn tells that the divine nurse, in order to render her charge, Demophon, immortal, secretly plunged him in the flames of the hearth every evening. This myth undoubtedly preserves in Greece the memory of very ancient sacrifices of new-born babies, who were thrown on the flames as victims to Moloch, to be like them reborn amongst the gods. Greek mysticism very quickly freed itself from the horrors of primitive magic, to which the Carthaginians remained obstinately attached. But this "Dionysian" aspect of the Greek spirit, awoken by contact with the East, in the capital of Ptolemy, attracted the Carthaginians much more than the rationalism of Socrates or Epicurus.

All the rural sanctuaries discovered on Cape Bon, the granary of Carthage, on the southern coast between Thinissut and Korba, and quite recently near Soliman on the north coast, contained a statue of Demeter. She was sometimes associated, as at Thinissut, with the divine masters of Carthage, Tanit and Ba'al, sometimes she retained her Sicilian paredroi, Persephone and Pluto, and sometimes she was surrounded by all the minor divinities of Eleusis. The statues at Korba, in a beautiful free classical style, were undoubtedly cast from moulds brought directly from Sicily during the fourth century. Another, much more archaic type—a face frozen under a line of small curls and a strange veil into the shape of a shell, surmounted by a tiara in the form of a shako, known as *polos*, a short body with breasts immediately under the neck, arms turned up at right angles near the belt—probably reproduced a very ancient icon. It may have been that of the Syracusan temple; its pillage in 396 B.C. had been expiated by establishing the cult at Carthage. But in Sicily, where the Greek

mythographers located the rape of Persephone by Pluto in the wild
volcanic mountains in the centre of the island, the triad formed by
the mother, daughter and undesirable son-in-law, had scarcely any
other function than to assure the fertility of the earth, as a result of
Persephone's return to daylight, after her winter sojourn in Hades.
Only at Eleusis was the agrarian ritual enriched by mystic interpretations. Here the hierophant gave information to the initiated which
enabled them to find the paths of salvation in the realm of the Dead
leading to the fields of bliss, where the initiates danced beneath the
leadership of Iacchos. But Ptolemy I had obtained permission from
the Eumolpide Timotheus to transplant the mysteries to a suburb
of Alexandria, baptised Eleusis for the occasion. This infringement
of rule forbidding the celebration of initiation outside Attica remained unique till the end of antiquity. It is very probable that the
Carthaginians, passing through Alexandria on business, might have
been initiated in the Egyptian Eleusis. Amongst the statuettes in the
sanctuaries of Soliman, there are certainly some that actually derive
from types created in the Ptolemaic capital. There is a large winged
dragon, which must have pulled Demeter's chariot, and a half-naked
goddess lying down representing the food-giving earth. As a result of
this enrichment, the religion of the Two Goddesses, as it is commonly
called, brought hope to Punic souls which they had not hitherto been
able to find in the national religion. This latter was very little concerned with the fate of the dead, except for those who had obtained
divinity by sacrificing their earthly bodies on the pyre. The others
undoubtedly had to be satisfied with a fairly miserable after-life,
either in the tomb itself or in a common dwelling, as devoid of attractions as the Sheol of the Hebrews or the Homeric Hades. Furthermore,
they were exposed to attack by demons, and attempts were made to
protect them by giving them amulets.

Hellenic mysticism obviously offered more consoling perspectives.
Its rapid diffusion is therefore not surprising, and is demonstrated by
changes in funeral customs. Bodies were often no longer buried but
incinerated in imitation of the Greeks. The protective images of the
Two Goddesses intertwined were placed beside them. Terra cotta
statuettes and curious painted steles, discovered in fairly large numbers
in Punic Sicily, represent the dead feasting around a well-stocked
table. This "banquet of immortality" symbolised the joys promised
to the initiated in the celestial dwelling, to which divine benevolence
henceforth admitted them. Moreover, Demeter was not the only
guarantor of their happiness. Another Greek god, Dionysos, who also
had his "mysteries", was introduced at Carthage, identifying himself

with an ancient Phoenician child-god, Shadrapa. As a result of this syncretism, Bacchus was intimately associated with Tanit and Ba'al Hammon and his attributes, the krater and ivy leaves, frequently appeared on the steles of the *tophet*. This was a new link with Alexandria, because Bacchism was a quasi-official religion in the realm of Ptolemy, where the sovereign himself was considered a new Dionysos.

The success of these more humane and more consoling religions at Carthage is certainly explained primarily by the social transformation that was taking place in the great Punic port. Its re-entry into commercial relations with Greece made it an international emporium, where a mixed population of sailors and adventurers grew up, very unwilling to accept the austere traditions of the sons of Dido and naturally tempted by a religion which was almost entirely indifferent to the old political and social frameworks. This Punic "plebs" would play a greater and greater part in the political life of Carthage, as will be seen. They also exercised a determining influence on its spiritual evolution. By an ingenious interpretation of strangely-formed vases, found in large numbers in the levels of the Carthaginian soil which correspond to the last days of the city, P. Cintas shows that on the eve of the final assault by Scipio, the besieged people were preparing to celebrate with great pomp a ceremony dedicated to Demeter. For this occasion, the priestesses wore receptacles on their heads containing the sacred fire and were surrounded by cupels containing grain offered to the goddess. It is significant that in the supreme test they placed their hopes as much on Greek goddesses, borrowed from their traditional enemies, as on the Dame who had watched over their destiny for centuries.

Carthage thus presents a strangely complex picture in the last two centuries of its life. The wild intransigence which enabled it to face the great peril of the fifth century had calmed down. A new civilisation, the fruit of Greek influence as much as of oriental traditions, was in process of being born. Flaubert felt and described this ambiguity very well, but carried away by his taste for the exotic, he undoubtedly laid too great a stress on the barbarous aspects of the "sombre Jerusalem". Certainly in many respects the Carthaginians remained orientals. They retained the eastern costume of a long tunic, worn plain by the common people, as is seen from a charming statuette at Carthage, or loaded with ornaments, to a greater or lesser degree, by the wealthy. Refinements borrowed from abroad did not cause the old customs to disappear from everyday life. Very soundly built cedar chests were found in the tombs of Byzacium, where the

Hellenistic steles from the tophet.

dry climate preserved the wood. These were used as cupboards before serving their owners as coffins. Such chests can still be found in peasant dwellings in Lebanon, as well as in many other Mediterranean countries. Phœnician language and writing defied Greek competition. But the modes of thought of Hannibal—the only Carthaginian whose personality is really known today—show that he too was open to many forms of Greek culture, which was rich enough for all men to be able to find something there to their advantage. Profiting both from the forces accumulated in the earlier period of withdrawal and from the life-giving co-operation of Hellenism, the Punic state in the beginning of the third century attained a power and prosperity it had never previously experienced.

The Greek geographer Strabo, who wrote in the first century A.D., estimated the population of the capital at 700,000 inhabitants at the time of the destruction. This number is certainly too high for the city alone, which never covered more than about 300 to 400 acres, even taking into account the congested plebeian families in six storey buildings. These were spaced out from the ports up to the summit of Byrsa, where there were possibly as many as 600 inhabitants per acre, as in the present day Casbah of Algiers. But the suburbs which extended over the whole peninsula as far as the outer defences, which cut the isthmus two and a half miles to the west of the summit of Byrsa, could have housed several hundred thousand men. Moreover most of them were undoubtedly peasants or market-gardeners, living by cultivating the numerous fields or gardens included in the fortified area. The number of non-agricultural workers remained quite low. The production capacity of the metallurgical and naval workshops can be measured approximately through the rearmament drive at the time of the final rupture with Rome in 146 B.C.: in one month 3,000 shields, 9,000 swords, 15,000 spears and 30,000 shafts for catapults were manufactured. These figures do not imply a very large number of workers. The greatest manufacturer of shields in Athens who kept about 700 articles in stock only employed 120 men. The total number of Carthaginian workers engaged in manufacturing arms can be estimated at about 3,000. A little later, the naval yards in two months improvised 50 galleys with three and five rows of oars, and 70 smaller boats. Assuming that a team of twenty men was employed for the construction of each boat and that two months were dedicated to the larger galleys and one month to the boats, a figure of 1,500 to 2,000 workmen is reached. It is known from Livy that the arsenals of Carthagena, obviously organised on the model of those of the metropolis, employed a total of 2,000 people. It is remarkable that despite the contingencies of siege, artisans of other trades were not requisitioned. The potters, in particular, must have worked up to the last day because their ovens have been found full, abandoned at the very moment of attack. As the products of their art were destined for the gods and the dead, it would undoubtedly have been judged sacrilegious to interrupt their activity.

Undoubtedly the very development of Carthage brought its growing pains. The régime established by the aristocracy in the fifth century found itself doubly threatened by the ambitions of the great, impatient with a strict discipline, and by the despair of the proletariat, reduced to poverty. But this proletariat comprised urban plebs, sailors, workmen, mercenaries and adventurers of all sorts, their numbers increased by the development of the town, as well as workers in the fields. These were for the most part of Libyan origin, and were reduced to a sort of serfdom by the large landowners. The discontent of these unfortunate people was all the more to be feared as they possessed considerable power. Mercenaries formed almost the whole of the army, and the peasants felt they were supported by the proximity of their kinsmen, the independent Libyans, who often carried their raids well into Punic territory. Social revolution was on the way, and the aspirants to dictatorship found themselves naturally inclined to take the leadership. The first attempt of this kind mentioned was led by Hanno the Great. Towards the middle of the fourth century he succeeded in raising 20,000 armed slaves and issued an appeal to the Libyans. The famous Mercenaries' War was also a social crisis, similar to the great revolts of the slaves which disturbed the East and Italy at about the same period. The Libyans rallied *en masse* to the side of the soldiers. The danger of a general revolution was so great at that time in the whole Mediterranean world that Rome did not take advantage of the occasion to overwhelm the enemy which she had had so much difficulty in fighting, and even gave them help. The same social solidarity, as much as patriotism, undoubtedly also prevented Hamilcar playing the rôle of Hanno. Nonetheless the victory, which was owed so much to his efforts, enabled him to put an end to the omnipotence of the oligarchy. According to Polybius, at the time of the second Punic War Carthage was much more democratic than Rome. The very conservative Greek historian did not hesitate to see in this political situation one of the causes of the defeat. It was however the democratic party, directed by the Barcides, who fought most energetically to safeguard the independence of their country, whereas the oligarchs on several occasions set an example of tedious compromises or of an equally unworthy prudence.

VI

THE DEATH OF CARTHAGE

THE decline of the Western Greeks and of the Etruscans was not fortuitous. Like so many other colonial empire builders they gave way beneath the pressure of the natives whom they themselves had taught and civilised. On the surface however it would appear that Carthage did not die from the attack of its own subjects but in a duel with another imperialist power over domination of the western Mediterranean. However, closer examination of the causes of its downfall shows that it resulted from the conjunction of Roman power with that of the Libyan realms, which could have resulted in the birth of a great autochthonous African state. The native actor certainly played no part in the first act of the drama of the death of Carthage. During the second, he assumed decisive importance, and the third was based entirely on the opposition of his ambitions to those of Rome.

To understand the fall of the western Phœnicians the historian must therefore find out the causes of both Roman superiority and the birth of a Libyan nation. The first of these problems is not within the province of this book. Moreover, the greatest minds since antiquity have tried to solve it, without complete success. A recent work by M. A. Aymard based on a particularly lucid and well-informed analysis sums up the present state of the question. Was the conflict fatal? Relations between Rome and Carthage were traditionally good. The poets later transposed this "honeymoon" into the myth of the love of Dido and Aeneas. When the Latin city had freed itself from the Etruscans at the end of the sixth century by expelling the Tarquins, Carthage thought it best not to leave a breach in its circle of alliances enclosing Greece. The treaty then concluded was renewed on several occasions and provided with clauses regulating the economic interests of the two parties. They were now the only great civilised powers in the western Mediterranean. But on the surface, their policies were in no way contradictory. The Roman Senate, composed of simple, down to earth men, never on any account envisaged engaging the legions overseas, and furthermore had only a few small ships at its disposal. As yet there were no business men in the Forum to exert any pressure in favour of competing with Punic commerce. The majority of the Punic aristocracy undoubtedly had no thought either of changing the traditional policy, based on mastery of the seas and the occupation of well-situated strategic bases. But ambitious men could be found thenceforth amongst generals and administrators who had fought and governed in Africa, encouraged by the easy submission of Sicily, who wanted to take advantage of the decline of the Greeks in Italy in order to substitute Punic domination everywhere for that of the Hellenes. Amongst the merchants also, there were some who calculated the increased profits that would accrue from this extension of the empire. Polybius expressly states that Rome felt threatened by Punic imperialism. However, this also resulted from pressure from the Italic peoples, who were attracted by the fertility of the Sicilian plains and whose actions often went beyond senatorial directives. The direct cause of the war was the occupation of Messina by a group of Campanian mercenaries.

Rome took the initiative from the start and retained it to the end, despite serious reverses. Its superior political genius and military organisation are even more striking in view of the lack of first-rate men for service in the war. It is particularly surprising to see this nation of landlubbers at one go and for ever capturing mastery of the seas from an adversary who had lived off its vessels for six centuries. It is generally known that this surprising reversal was the work of the Consul C. Duilius, with the aid of a very simple invention which immobilised the enemy ships by the use of boarding-bridges fitted with grapnels. This episode provides a guide to the psychological structure of the two adversaries. Duilius's solution, despite its efficiency, was beneath the dignity of a true sailor. It undoubtedly represents a regression in the art of naval strategy—which the Greeks had brought to great perfection—because it renders void the very *raison d'être* of a boat: its rapidity and its manoeuvrability. Moreover, Roman pilots were always rather poor and the great defeats their fleets encountered were due much more to their ignorance of the sea and the islands than to the ability of their enemies. But Roman commonsense cared little for elegance. Presented with a new difficulty, it did not try to assimilate the proper techniques for solving the problem but rather to discover the most simple method to meet an already known situation.

On the other hand it would be surprising that the Carthaginians allowed themselves to be left at the mercy of this elementary stratagem, if archaeology had not already shown their absolute technical incapacity. This incapacity is all the more remarkable when it is remembered that Archimedes, the greatest of the very few ancient

57] A stuccoed pilaster in Hellenistic style, discovered at the tophet in Carthage.

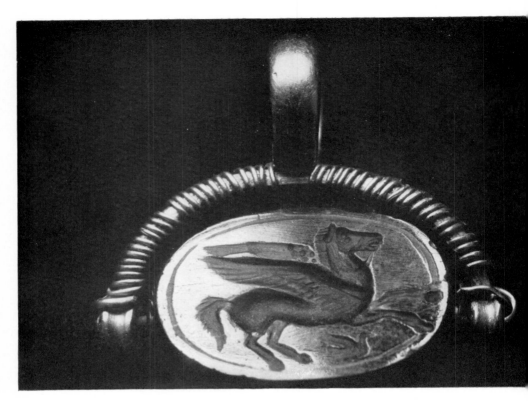

[58] Hellenistic scarab, from Utica: Pegasus.

[59] Neo-Punic chapel to Demeter discovered at Thuburbo Majus; example of Punic Hellenistic architecture.

[60] Prophylactic mask of a man in glass paste (*photo Bouchoucha*).

[61] Mask of a woman (*photo Bouchoucha*).

[62] Punic sarcophagus discovered in the same necropolis as Ill. 63, preserved in the Louvre. The model of these sarcophagi came from Etruria. The statue most probably represents a god rather than the deceased. (First half of the third century B.C.).

[63] Sarcophagus "of the priestess" (third century B.C.): Tanit clad in a robe imitating a bird's skin.

[64] Gargoyle in the form of a lion's head. Compare with the lion from Mactar in Ill. 89.

[65] Terra cotta statue of Demeter from the sanctuary of Soliman. Archaist work, from the beginning of the Christian era. The head derives from a fifth century Greek prototype. Notice the deformation of the anatomy (breasts, arms brought back at right angles). The head-dress is identical with that on the following statue.

[66] Demeter discovered in a rural sanctuary in the neighbourhood of Korba (reconstructed by L. Poinssot and L. Brechot). Notice the stiff shell-shaped veil on which stands the chimney-shaped pillar. This stiff veil characterises African images of Demeter and Koré. The work, in a much freer style than the preceding one, must have been moulded from a Greek statue from Sicily.

[67] Statue of Koré from the same place. The goddess holds a young pig, like the Eleusinian initiates who brought the animal from Athens to Eleusis to sacrifice it.

[68] Statue of Pluto from the same sanctuary.

[69] Greek statue of Demeter, discovered at Carthage in a cache where polytheistic worshippers hid the statues of their gods to save them from the "sacrilege" committed by the Christians at the end of the fourth century A.D. Judging from the arrangement of the draperies, this work, or its prototype, dates from the fourth century A.D.

[70] Statuette from Carthage, representing a dedicant. The costume consists only of a long, very simple robe, similar to the clothing of the Arabs. The simplicity of its lines gives the work a vigour which puts it into the class of the best products of Punic art. Notice the ecstatic expression of the face.

[71] Statuette from Carthage. Complex female costume found again in the Neo-Punic period. Over a long, very fine robe is worn a pleated dress, raised at the waist and extending as far as the knees. It is covered by a sort of pleated apron, with a long embroidered band round it (compare with the Greek statuette in Ill. 10). There is a sort of shawl on the shoulders.

[72] Coffin-chest in cedar wood, originating from a Punic tomb at Byzacium (third to second century).

[73] The Punic "Mars". The image of a horseman god, undoubtedly Hadad, whose exploits were described in the epic poems of Ugarit in the 14th century B.C. This god was worshipped at Carthage from its origin. The legend according to which the site of Byrsa was chosen because of the discovery of a horse's head is related to his cult. He was also represented on Carthaginian money by means of the horse shown at the foot of a palm tree. Here he wears a pointed helmet, of oriental origin, found again on the steles at Cirta, and carries a sort of military ensign.

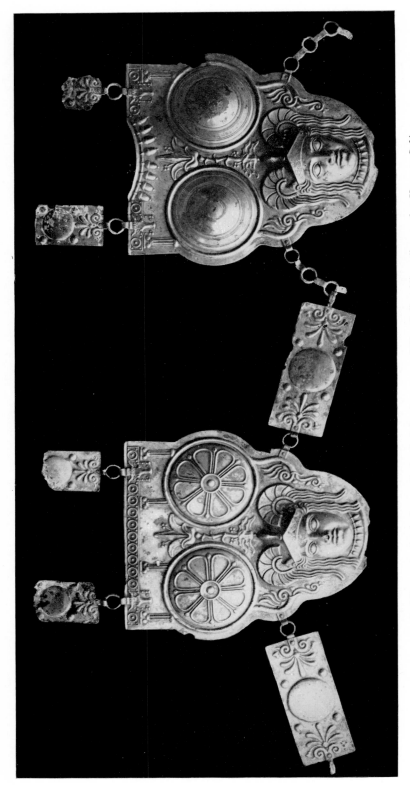

[74] Campanian breastplate, undoubtedly belonging to one of Hannibal's soldiers, discovered at Ksour es Saf in the Sahel. It was found in a wooden coffin similar to that in Ill. 72, with the sword-belt of the dead man.

scholars able to draw practical applications from scientific theory, lived at Syracuse, their ally at the beginning of the war. The Carthaginians are often said to have made advances in naval techniques, and it has even been supposed that they discovered secrets in this sphere which were lost after their fall. Their impotence when confronted with Duilius's boarding bridges makes it difficult to believe that the ability of their builders was based on anything but routine tradition.

It is tempting to explain the defeat of Carthage on land by the superiority of the Italian national army, which Rome had already formed, over the expatriate mercenaries of its adversary. However, the defeat of Regulus and the victorious resistance of Hamilcar at Eryx in the last years of the conflict prove that the professional soldier was not necessarily inferior to the legionary. Carthage was more than anything else the victim of its archaic conception of command. Up to the end of the fifth century, all the Mediterranean cities had organised armies of citizens commanded by their magistrates, animated by patriotism and governed by civilian discipline. The Hellenic professional armies could not summon up such sentiments. The lure of gain and taste for adventure could not give birth to an *esprit de corps*—in fact this rested entirely on the mystique of the leader. The Greek cities had rapidly to abandon command to the condottieri who obtained absolute devotion from their men by inspiring them with religious confidence in their good luck. In the eyes of these fanatical troops their leader possessed supernatural power, emanating directly from the divinity who guaranteed his triumph. This supernatural good luck could be a source of political power. In fact, the Hellenic kings were only soldiers who had proved their right to rule by victory. Obviously the Punic oligarchy could not put itself in the hands of one of these adventurers. But it was wrong to believe that its mercenaries could be led by officers chosen from amongst its own members, whose prestige furthermore, it destroyed by exercising the most jealous supervision. Four of these unfortunate men perished on the cross during the war for having sustained defeat. Those who escaped the judges often fell beneath the blows of their own soldiers. Carthage only realised its mistake when its very life was endangered. When Regulus encamped beneath its walls, it resigned itself to delegating command to a foreigner, the Spartan Xanthippus, who saved it. After his victory, moreover, the Spartan had the good sense to return home. But a great revolt by the mercenaries almost immediately showed that it was impossible to re-establish the old military régime. By abdicating its authority to Hamilcar Barca, the Carthaginian oligarchy resigned itself to recognising a personal power freed from all control, which turned

13

the foreign policy of the Republic into completely new channels.

The principate of the Barca family, passed by Hamilcar to his son-in-law Hasdrubal and then to his son Hannibal, lasted for nearly fifty years. It is certainly reminiscent of the authority the Mago family exercised in the sixth century. The spirit of the great adventurer captains, Hanno and Himilco, lives again in these creators of an Empire. But more than anything else they were men of their own time, formed in the Alexandrian mould. Their power rested on an army made up of men of all origins and organised in the Greek manner. Like the Macedonian kings, a general of the Barca clan possessed political power derived immediately from his military authority and justified by the very success of his enterprises. In the Saguntum incident, which was the cause of the second Punic war, Hannibal took sole responsibility for attacking the town, a decision which the Punic Senate was content to approve by accepting its consequences. It was Hannibal again who concluded an alliance with Philip V of Macedon in 216 B.C. Polybius has preserved the text of this alliance: the senators present at Headquarters bound the entire assembly by their signature which followed the general's. The purely military origin of this power is evident in the appointment of its holder, who was acclaimed by the army itself without any intervention from the metropolis. It confined itself to confirming the choice and then delegating some of its senators to stay with the general in the position of auxiliaries, not supervisors. The choice of soldiers always fell to a Barcid, which leads one to suppose that they believed in the heredity of charism—that is a supernatural predisposition to victory—in the family. Dynastic legitimacy in Hellenic lands was based on similar principles. Moreover, it may be conjectured that Hamilcar and his successors accredited the belief to the supernatural origin of their good fortune. They particularly worshipped Melqart of Gades, whom Hannibal consulted before leaving on his great expedition. But this monarchical tendency was foreign to the tradition of authentic Punic religion. It accorded better with the mentality of the Iberians, who seem to have believed in the supernatural power of their kings, particularly the "providentialism" of the Hellenic Basileis. The logical consequence of this evolution would have been the creation of a military régime in Spain, which would have been advantageous to the Barcids. It is possible that Hasdrubal envisaged this: from the almost sacrilegious audacity which made him call the town he founded Qart Hadasht (which it still retains today in the form of Carthagena) it may be supposed that he planned to transport the seat of Empire to this third Tyre, ruled from the sumptuous palace he built. It will be recalled that Forrer has shown that Qart means capital as well as town.

The Barcids were not only related to Alexander and his successors by the nature of their power and the organisation of their army. Their policy in Spain is much more reminiscent of Macedonian imperialism than previous Carthaginian enterprises. When Hamilcar assumed power after the Mercenaries' War, economic distress caused the recent successes to be forgotten. The loss of Sardinia, ravaged by Rome with the help of civil war, was added to that of Sicily. A war indemnity of over 13 million gold francs and the accumulated debts of almost thirty years had to be paid off. The ruin of the state resulted in the ruin of private individuals. The necropolis of the Odeon which dates from that time, and the upper layers of the *tophet*, contain only miserable offerings, and the costly products of eastern industry are lacking.

The poverty of Carthage, more than all diplomatic controls, deprived it of the means to undertake its revenge. But it was recalled that the conquest of the hinterland states and the great expeditions of Hanno and Himilco had previously enabled the republic rapidly to efface the effects of Himera. The country which could supply the resources necessary for Punic recovery on this occasion was unanimously agreed: Spain, at all times the principal source of wealth for the western Phœnicians, still concealed enormous, incompletely exploited, reserves in iron, copper and silver mines, and fertile plains. Its inhabitants, once disciplined, would make excellent soldiers. But to be profitable, conquest must be total and rapid. However, it had taken Carthage several centuries to conquer in Africa a territory five or six times smaller than the Iberian peninsula. Every circumstance therefore forced Hamilcar to replace the traditional methods of Carthaginian generals by those which enabled Alexander to conquer the Persian empire in ten years. The story is told that when Hannibal, at the end of his life, was taking refuge in Asia he met Scipio, and the two old generals amicably discussed their profession. Invited to class in order of merit the great captains of the past, the Carthaginian gave first place to Alexander, second to Pyrrhus of Epirus. The anecdote remains instructive, even if purely fictional, which is probable. Hannibal admired the Macedonian for having dispersed multitudes with not very numerous troops, and reached the limits of the known world. This simple formula contains the fundamental principle of the strategy he borrowed from him: the concentration of all available forces in a shock troop of limited size, and then the rational determination of the breaking points where the action of this human battering-ram would bring about the enemy's collapse; finally, as a result of the extreme mobility of this assault group, the extension of the limits of the theatre of operations as far as was necessary to annihilate the reserves of the adversary and prevent the reassembly of his forces. The efficiency of these tactics, which are similar to those employed by the Mongol conquerors in the Middle Ages and which with the use of tanks has been brought down to present-day usage, was first demonstrated by Hamilcar and Hasdrubal, and in eighteen years enabled Carthage to conquer all the country to the south of the Ebro.

Hannibal surpassed all his masters in genius. The nineteenth century German scholars saw the events at Cannae as the origin of modern strategy, when the leader continued to manoeuvre even during the course of an action, instead of being content to order his dispositions in advance and leave the battle to prove their value. But this discovery, the consequences of which were undoubtedly not entirely understood by its author himself, as he did not try to use it in the other wars he directed, can no more be considered the fruit of the Punic spirit than were the artistic creations of Hellenic Carthage, or the philosophical works of Hasdrubal who settled at Athens under the name of Clitomachus and eventually became the leader of the Stoic school there. Hannibal, as far as strategy was concerned, was a Greek, formed by Greek masters. He would not have found it at all difficult in the last twenty years of his life to resume his former profession of condottiere under Antiochus and Prusias. The influence of Alexander on the Barca family undoubtedly explains an astonishing paradox in their strategic concept—which was not the least cause of Hannibal's defeat. Although, till then, all Carthaginian policy had been based on mastery of the sea, neither Hamilcar nor his son made a serious effort to regain from the Roman fleet the supremacy it retained almost without a struggle till the end of the second Punic War. Thus Hannibal preferred to arrive in Italy at the end of a five-months march across wild country, which cost him half his army. Such expeditions were very much in the tradition of Alexander, which an illustrious contemporary, the Seleucid Antiochus the Great, had just repeated by penetrating as far as the frontier of India. Undoubtedly a landing on the Italian coasts would have been hazardous in 218. But later, the absence of a navy deprived Hannibal of reinforcements from Spain, caused the death of his brother, Hasdrubal, and the destruction of his army, and finally wiped out the most important diplomatic consequences of the battle of Cannae: the alliance with Philip V of Macedon, which, if it had been followed by effective co-operation, would undoubtedly have been enough to alter the outcome of the war. The construction of a large fleet would not have been an impossible undertaking for Carthage, which then had at its disposal the arsenals with which Hasdrubal had endowed Carthage, in addition to its own. This astonishing omission, in a sphere which Carthage had until then considered essential, caused Roman historians to think that his native land deliberately supported Hannibal poorly. S. Gsell rightly contests this theory. Hannibal, in fact, wittingly decided to renounce naval warfare by virtue of the very principles of his strategy. Rome, a continental power, could only be completely conquered on land. But this calculation was only valid in circumstances where a victory could be obtained very rapidly. Rome, having succeeded in continuing the war after the destruction of its principal armies, resumed the initiative as a result of Fabius' delaying tactics. By dint of avoiding decisive encounters, Fabius finally succeeded in immobilising Hannibal in Capua. Thereafter, Hannibal found himself in the position of a chess-player who has pushed his queen too boldly into the enemy lines. The issue depended on the routes followed by reinforcements, and here Rome possessed the advantage because of its naval superiority and the difficulty of the overland route across Gaul.

Another disadvantage of Hellenic strategy was the superficiality of the conquests attained by these picked troops, who skated over the surface of immense human masses, smoothing over all obstacles, without ever penetrating the depths. The facility with which Scipio made himself master of Spain in three campaigns, proves that the natives, who soon gave the legions unpleasant proof of their warlike qualities, regarded the change of masters with indifference. The deepest traces of Phœnician influence in ancient Iberian culture are much rather the fruit of centuries of commerce between the Latin trading stations and the interior, than of the startling Barca epic. The mysterious Lady of Elché, whose face beneath a barbarous headdress preserves the purity and power of early Greek classicism, remains isolated in her perfection—so remote from the banal vulgarity of Carthaginian art that S. Gsell was possibly right in denying her any affinity with it. The least controversial traces of Hannibal's passage are found in France. The acropolis of Enserune, between Narbonne and Beziers, contains the huts and tombs of an Iberian tribe, supplied by Marseilles and Empories with the products of Greek industry. A few tombs from the third century contained religious objects which are definitely of Punic origin. They included two busts of Demeter, intended for burning perfumes, which are exactly similar to those which contained the *favissa* of Santa Monica, a small mask of polychrome glass, and particularly a terra cotta plaquette, representing Ba'al Hammon on his throne, in a ritual attitude. These objects, all from the same period, could neither have been brought by ordinary trade, because no other current product of Carthaginian industry is found with them, nor can they have been used for the devotions of the natives, whose rites show no sign of conversion to the Phœnician religion. They must therefore have served the devotion of a Punic group established in the village, at a date necessarily somewhere between the breaking of the treaty of 226 B.C., which confined the enterprises of the Barca chiefs to the south of the Ebro, and Scipio's counter-offensive. It would thus appear probable that Hannibal made a base at Enserune and quartered a garrison there.

The battle of Baecula, which gave Spain to Scipio, and the defeat of the desperate attempt by Hasdrubal the younger to join his brother in Italy, definitively settled the fate of Barca imperialism between 208 and 206 B.C. As Carthage had lost hope of preserving the hegemony in some form in the western Mediterranean, the only question now was if it would be able to survive as the capital of an African state. In short, its destiny thus depended on the remarkably stable and very characteristic laws which governed the political evolution of the Maghreb.

For the first time, then, sociological phenomena appeared in that kind of autonomous continent between sea and desert, which were to be reproduced without notable change there until the end of the Middle Ages or even until the present day. These laws of evolution of Berber societies were formulated in the fourteenth century A.D. by the great historian of the race, Ibn Khaldoun, with such lucidity that his Prolegomena frequently even elucidate the history of antiquity, of which he had only very imperfect knowledge.

The geographical and human conditions governing the development of Berber societies have already been studied. The region conquered by the Carthaginians, which covered barely a tenth of the total surface of the Maghreb, was the only part of that area which was not powerfully defended against foreign influences—on the contrary the situation of its coasts encouraged easy relations with the east. Therefore close political or at least cultural ties often bind it to the east.

Thus Carthage was to be followed by the Aghlabite Emirate, the Egypto-Maghrebi régime of the Fatimides and finally the Turkish Regency. But attempts by the orientals to widen their domination towards the west generally came up against the xenophobia of the Libyan-Berber natives. The Saharan tribes, whose standard of life and culture is scarcely higher even today than the poorest populations of the polar regions or the tropical forests, only intervened in this struggle in a purely negative fashion, by savage destruction, whenever occasion offered, of the towns and cultures of the settled inhabitants. On the other hand, the tribes of the Algerian Tell, and particularly Morocco, who were settled agriculturalists, formed strange political systems, for which all current sociological terminology appears inadequate. A more numerous or better endowed clan than the rest quickly imposes its hegemony over a frequently very extensive territory, and runs it as common property under the authority of the oldest member, who divides the privileges and burdens of power among his relations. The death of this patriarch often gives rise to bitter quarrels, which put the clan at a disadvantage compared with its rivals, and when this process is repeated over several generations, the clan's energy is at last exhausted and it becomes extinct.

These "Empire-building" tribes came most frequently, both in antiquity and the Middle Ages, from the western part of the Maghreb, so that Africa was then divided between two powers: one autochthonous, originating in Morocco, the other of oriental foundation, with Tunisia as its centre. The first Libyan "State" appeared at Morocco about the fourth century B.C., founded by the tribe of the Moors. The Masaesylii, masters in the third century of the greater part of the Algerian Tell, between the Moulouya and the Oued el Kebir, which flows into the sea not far from Philippeville, may also have come from Morocco. The Massylii, who possibly originated in the Aures region, were at first content with the remainder of Constantine, but were quick to take advantage of the weakening of Carthage to extend their domain at its expense in the Greater Tunisian Tell. Masaesylii and Massylii seemed to the foreigners to be two branches of the same nation, the Numidians, and the kings born to each clan very quickly sought to dominate the other. These rivalries were to decide the fate of Carthage.

At the time of Hannibal, Gaia reigned over the Massylii and Syphax over the Masaesylii. In general, Carthage supported the first of these princes, which incited Syphax to seek an alliance with Scipio, when the latter had conquered Spain. But the death of Gaia upset these alliances. Syphax took advantage of the quarrels among the candidates for the throne to seize the neighbouring realm by driving out Massinissa, the son of Gaia, who had triumphed over his rivals. He had been encouraged and supported by the governor of the Punic hinterland states, Hasdrubal, the son of Gisgo (who must not be confused with his Barca namesake). As a better guarantee of the alliance Hasdrubal gave him his daughter Sophonisba in marriage. She was much younger than her husband, very beautiful, endowed with a

charm and spirit which no man could withstand, well educated into
the bargain, and a good musician. The Carthaginian lady was soon
the real ruler of the unified Numidian realm.

But Massinissa had managed to escape his enemy. He sought
refuge on Mount Bellus which overlooks Hippo Regius, today Bône.
These mountains of La Khoumirie are covered with very thick forest,
which today is still wild and difficult to penetrate, haunted by the
savage beasts which previously abounded there, and at all times a
perfect refuge for outlaws. The fugitive prince was able to gather
together a few companions who lived off their flocks, by hunting and
particularly by pillaging, preferably on Punic territory, which was
richer and less well guarded than Numidian country. Pestered by
these "fellagha", the Carthaginians invited Syphax to get rid of them.
The "caid" Bucar, charged with this task, almost succeeded. The
brigands were attacked from all sides, deprived of their flocks and
their tents, surrounded in a gorge and pitilessly massacred. Massinissa
however escaped, with fifty or so horsemen. But he was immediately
pursued and wounded, losing all except four of his companions in
the chase. The five fugitives arrived at the banks of a great river,
undoubtedly the Medjerda, continually hunted by their enemies.
Preferring death to the fate awaiting them if captured they threw
themselves without hesitation into the waters, which were swollen
by the floods. Two of them and all the horses were carried away by
the current. The Massaesylii, believing all of them drowned, turned
and left. But Massinissa, despite his wound, was able to swim to the
bank, helped by two faithful companions, and hid with them in the
undergrowth. He took refuge in a cavern, where he stayed for a long
time, treating his wound with herbs and fed by his companions who
stole from the douars of the neighbourhood.

The Massylii were not happy, however, under the subjugation
of Syphax. A rumour began to spread that the legitimate king was
not dead. One fine day he reappeared, still scarcely cured, only just
able to sit on his horse, and surrounded by forty warriors he had
rallied together. Within a few hours, his tribe rose in his support.
With six thousand men on foot or on horseback, he recovered his
kingdom without a blow being struck and began to overrun the lands
of the Carthaginians and Syphax. Meanwhile, Syphax had rallied his
forces. A great battle took place between Cirta and Hippo, and
Massinissa was again conquered. Once more he was an outlaw and
fugitive with a following of sixty horsemen, closely pursued by
Vermina, the son of Syphax. This time it was the south that received
him, the arid mountains of the Tripolitanian Sahara. He resumed his

lawless life, ceaselessly on the alert, obliged to ride interminably to outwit his pursuers. Syphax left no stone unturned to capture him and would certainly have succeeded if the wandering king had not seen Roman ships appear while camping by the sea one day. Their commander was Laelius, the friend of Scipio. He warned the Numidians to hold themselves ready. Publius had been elected consul and given the task of attacking Africa. The expedition was hastily prepared in Sicilian ports.

In the summer of 205 B.C., Scipio embarked an army of around 35,000 men at Libybaeum (today Marsala), on 400 troop-ships escorted by 40 galleys. The Carthaginians could do nothing to prevent either the crossing or the landing—which proceeded unhampered to the north of the estuary of the Medjerda, very near Utica. Massinissa and his few warriors immediately joined the Romans. All Carthaginian hopes rested on Syphax. It appears that the Italian and particularly the Spanish compaigns had exhausted all the military resources of the republic. The king did actually come to its aid but after suffering two defeats he returned discouraged to Cirta. Massinissa then prevailed upon Scipio to put a detachment commanded by Laelius at his disposal. Thus supported, he easily re-conquered his kingdom for the third time, and then repaired to Cirta (Constantine) the capital of his rival. In the battle which took place beneath its walls, Syphax was completely conquered and taken prisoner.

Massinissa entered the palace as a conqueror—and then met Sophonisba. The queen threw herself at his feet, begging him not to give her up to the Romans. Her overwhelming beauty and charm instantly awoke such violent passion in the heart of the Numidian (very ardent in love as all his race, according to Livy) that he insisted on marrying her without a moment's delay. But the Romans understood the ability of the daughter of Hasdrubal too well to risk losing the whole profit of a campaign through consideration for an ally's feelings. Scipio refused to recognise the marriage and demanded that Sophonisba be handed over to him, as a captive and as the property of the Roman people. Massinissa withdrew into his tent and for a while allowed his grief free play. Then he called a slave and sent a cup of poison to the Carthaginian girl. Sophonisba died without a murmur, thinking perhaps of Dido and the native land which she too had served to the point of the supreme sacrifice.

The loss of Numidia destroyed the last hope of Carthage. Thirty senators came to kiss the feet of Scipio at his General Headquarters at Tunis and to beg for peace—which he did not refuse. But while the plenipotentiaries were leaving for Rome to negotiate with the

Senate, it was learned that Hannibal had landed at Hadrumetum. He brought back the remains of the army that had made Rome tremble for sixteen years without a single defeat. It is most moving to find on Tunisian soil the relics of one of his soldiers who undoubtedly died during the landing, before the supreme defeat. On February 20, 1909, a funeral cave was opened near Ksour Es Saf, a village situated about forty miles south of Susa. It contained a breast-plate almost as new as when it left the armourers, as well as the cedar-wood sarcophagi already mentioned. The breast-plate is composed of two heart-shaped pieces, identically decorated, one to cover the back, the other the chest. Below, there is a head of Minerva, full-face, wearing a helmet, framed by a mane falling symmetrically from a double crest. The stem of some sort of thistle, ending in a fleuron which seems to rise from the crest of the helmet, separates two discs, decorated on the breast-plate with a rosette with eight petals. The date and origin of the armour are indisputable. In the third century B.C. only the workshops of Campania manufactured these strange breast-plates, in shape and decoration more suited to the parade ground than to war. The muse of history, who does not encourage flights of imagination from those who serve her, might perhaps not approve of the picture this conjures up: the soldier of Byzacium, enrolled in the great Barcid army when very young, a veteran of Spain and Gaul, of Trasimene and Cannae, who returned at last to die in his own country, but who wanted to have with him in his tomb the armour he had bought at Capua, when the fortunes of his leader were already declining, arranged according to ancestral rites.

The return of Hannibal awoke the patriotism of the Punic masses who were already provoked by famine. The war had destroyed the harvests, and Scipio who controlled supplies to the capital from Tunis, deducted the lion's share for his army. In their exaltation, the Carthaginians went to scarcely justifiable excesses. They forcibly seized a stranded Roman convoy and attacked the boat of the deputies who had come to protest against this outrage. Moreover it was not absolutely absurd to hope to drive out the invader. Vermina, son of Syphax, remained in the Masaesylian state and was most anxious for revenge on Massinissa. Hannibal immediately understood that the fate of the war depended yet again on the changing fortunes of the Numidian kings. A glance at the map of Tunisia shows that the strategic key to the country lies in the mountains of the High Tell separating the plains of the Medjerdah from the Kairouann steppes. During the last World War, French troops in Tunisia, too weak to prevent the German landing, retired to these heights in November

1943, while awaiting the arrival of the Anglo-American forces. Control of the backbone sheltered the allies from the thrusts of Rommel's army, while waiting to launch the offensive on Tunis. The central part of this very scattered mountainous area consists of the plateau of Mactar, overlooking the fertile plains of Siliana, Sers and further east, of Mellègue. The master of this retreat is in the fortunate position of being able to strike both in the direction of Sahel and towards the north, in the direction of Carthage. There, the Massylian realm with its capital of Zama had grown up. Hannibal realised that if he once again succeeded in driving out Massinissa he would hold Scipio in check beneath the walls of Carthage. Therefore, he left Hadrumetum, moved eastwards and established his camp outside Zama. There is still a great deal of uncertainty regarding the site of this famous town, which is irritating for the historian. At least two towns bore the name of Zama. One of them can definitely be identified with a modern village, still called Jama. But it is not known whether it is in any way connected with the royal city. It is likely that it was, although the position of the town is rather difficult to fit in with the indications on Roman maps, and its hilly site does not correspond well with the description by Sallust of a lowland town, fortified by men but not by nature. Some years ago it seemed as if the enigma was solved by the discovery of two Latin inscriptions bearing the name of Zama, in some ruins about seven miles south of Jama. But excavations at the site revealed one of those traps chance sometimes likes to lay for scholars. Here was a village subordinate to Zama, named Maraci, not the town itself. However, scarcely half a mile from the ruin is a strange monument, perhaps the most mysterious ever found on African soil. It is an enormous carved-stone mass, 150 feet long, 50 feet wide, and 18 feet high, divided by two stairways leading to the summit; it is undoubtedly a monumental altar, of comparable proportions and shape to the one which decorated the sanctuary of Zeus at Pergamum or the altar dedicated to Zeus Eleutherios by Hieron II, King of Syracuse. Excavations in 1949 revealed a round shield sculptured in bas-relief, showing a beautiful profile of Artemis with a quiver amongst the other elements of the frieze of arms and trophies decorating the façade.

The building certainly commemorates a victory. But particular features of the decoration and architectural structure make it possible to establish that it was only constructed in the first century B.C. And in 46 B.C., Zama was once more the scene of dramatic events. It was then the capital of King Juba I, who had thrown in his lot with the Roman republicans who had fled to Africa after the death of

Pompey. Caesar pursued them and conquered them at Thapsus, together with their Numidian ally. The Numidian king proclaimed to his subjects that in the event of defeat he himself would burn with them, transforming the town into a vast funeral pyre. Undoubtedly by so doing he intended to revive the Punic tradition of the supreme sacrifice of the king, adopted by the Numidians when they were converted to the Phœnician religion. But the Zamians cared little for such honour. When they heard the news of Thapsus, they closed their doors and forced Juba to undertake a less spectacular suicide. He fled to one of his castles and fought a duel to the death in single combat with a Roman friend. Caesar came to Zama, granted it liberty in recompense for rallying to his side and allowed it to retain its rank as capital of the new province cut out of the Numidian realm. The monumental altar was undoubtedly built as a thank-offering for the safety of the city. The choice of site, several miles from the town, near a pass uniting the two basins to the fertile plains, the valleys of the Siliana and the Assuras, was possibly determined by the memory of the great battle which delivered Africa into Roman hands.

No ancient text mentions the monument, which is not so surprising as there is no complete geographical description of Roman Africa available. At the time of the Arab conquest its significance was obviously forgotten, but its imposing and unusual shape gave rise to one of the mythical explanations which very easily satisfy popular imagination in every country. In this case a monstrous giant, named Klib, was thought to lie beneath the altar, thenceforth called Kbor Klib—"the tomb of Klib". This fantastic cavalier had a mount of comparable size, which he attached to a no less monumental post— in fact, the tower-shaped mausoleum of a notable citizen of Maraci— by a golden chain which was so long that the steed, depending on whether he pulled to the West or the East, could crop the grass in the lands of Assuras or drink in those of Siliana. A few leagues away to the south-east stand the grandiose ruins of the Roman colony of Assuras, founded by Tiberius—a temple and a theatre amongst them, which have not yet been explored. The story-tellers had no difficulty in making them the residence of a sister of Klib who, learning of her brother's death, hastened to bury him, laden with a basket of sand which she emptied when she saw that the tomb was already constructed. This so the tale goes, was the origin of a yellow mound which stands in sharp contrast to the dark soil of the plain of Assuras. It is amusing to discover a similar folk-lore theme at Athens explaining the formation of the Lycabettus.

The disproportionate enthusiasm of Carthage at the return of

Hannibal was born of the hope that the conqueror of Cannae would again gather all the resources of his genius to save his native land. This hope was disappointed. No student of strategy would seek instruction from events at Zama. Hannibal and Scipio took up the ordinary dispositions of good generals of the time. The lack of homogeneity of the Punic army, which Hannibal had utilised to his advantage at Cannae, this time caused his defeat.

Carthage conquered was nothing more than a pawn. The destiny of Africa depended henceforth on Numidian skill in unifying it. But Rome knew all too well the danger that a great African state represented for her to allow even Massinissa to put the economic resources of the old Tyrian metropolis at the disposal of a young and new nation. The hypocrisy of two policies, both equally unscrupulous, thus reigned supreme during the decline of the unfortunate city. It opposed them with a dignity and courage which compel admiration. Not wishing to admit their rivalry, Rome and Massinissa pretended that they continued to fear a Punic uprising, though they knew this to be impossible. For the fifty years of his long reign the Numidian incessantly nibbled away at the territory which the treaty of 201 B.C. had limited by the "Phœnician trench", cutting Tunisia obliquely from Tabarka to Sfax. He reckoned that in the town itself there were partisans sufficiently far-sighted to prefer the survival of their civilisation to illusory freedom. Rome forbade Carthage to defend itself. Inspired by the ferocious realism of the elder Cato, it waited until its supposed ally would be at its mercy as a defenceless victim. The occasion came in 150 B.C. The democratic party, opposed to Massinissa, dragged Carthage into a war where she was conquered. With savage cruelty, the Senate prepared its forces for the final stroke, without wanting to hear the Punic side of the story. Carthage still hoped to move the Senate to pity: it condemned nationalist leaders to death and agreed unconditionally to complete disarmament. The consuls thought they had the city at their mercy and pronounced the death sentence: the Carthaginians were to abandon their town and go and settle ten miles away in the interior of the country. But the Senate reckoned without the fundamental and irrepressible vitality which still lay in these desperate people. The doors were closed in the face of the legions. New arms were improvised. As incompetent as they were pitiless, Manilius and Censorinus fought on land and sea. For three years, Carthage resisted without real hope.

But closely blockaded, the town of Dido still remained a formidable retreat. Polybius, who was present at the last battles, described the triple fortifications of the isthmus in minute detail, the interior wall, so high and so wide that its base served as barracks and arsenal, sheltering the war machines and the elephants; the second rampart and the first line, consisting of a ditch and a stockade. For a century, archaeologists searched in vain on every side of the ruins for earth works, the mass of which could not, they believed, have been completely demolished along with the walls. It was in fact General R. Duval, commander of the French troops in Tunisia, who discovered the only indestructible remains in 1949, from an aeroplane: the enormous trench of the exterior line, 65 feet wide, which cuts the rock of the isthmus at right angles, a league from Byrsa. Behind, a ridge of sandstone still bears the scars left by the stakes which supported the wooden observation posts where the sentinels watched. Another piece of evidence still remains at sea, at the point of Salammbo: a rectangular terreplein which served as an advanced landing stage at the exit of the ports. On this *choma*—as the Greeks called it—Scipio Aemilianus succeeded in establishing a bridge-head, by constructing an enormous jetty from the beach of La Goulette, which blocked the channel of the port.

Rome had finally found a leader whose human qualities, no less than his military ability, obliterated the baseness and mediocrity of his predecessors. Adopted grandson of the great Scipio, the son of Aemilius Paulus who had conquered Macedonia, Scipio Aemilianus already possessed the nobility of heart and spiritual worth which would one day make the Roman aristocracy, regenerated by Hellenism, worthy of governing a peaceful world. His humanism did not prevent him torturing Carthage, but enabled him to understand the horror of the task which he had to undertake. Polybius saw him weep at the sight of the fire he had ordered to be lit and heard him recite verses by Homer: "One day also Holy Troy will perish, and Priam and the people of Priam of the good spear". Perhaps, he said to his friend, another man would repeat them one day about his own country. It is undoubtedly possible to find this remorse idle and tinged with national egoism. But the historian must remember that present-day moral values were built up slowly, and pay homage to all those capable of progressing, however minutely, beyond the standards current in their circle and in their times.

The last act of the death of Carthage has also left moving traces in the soil. Excavators have gathered stone bullets from twenty places in the city, accumulated by the defenders or thrown by machines during battle. When the superposition of strata was carefully observed, a thick bed of ashes was found covering the floors of houses. The structure of these houses and of the objects such as lamps and coins which have been found in them, enable them to be dated from the last Punic period. In these ashes, Ch. Saumagne found a fine female head in ivory, protected by a magma of iron, resulting from the fusion by fire of the nails of the chest in which it was enclosed. This curio gives some idea of the treasures which the conquerors must have recovered from the ruins, part of which they gave up to the Greeks in Sicily as reparation for the pillages which their towns had in the past suffered. The workshop where the potters made small objects to accompany the dead is situated at the entrance of the necropolis of Dermech. In 1901 P. Gauckler discovered brick firing-chambers still full of the pottery, already baked, which the artist had not been able to take out on that spring day in 146 B.C., when Scipio attacked. Amidst the lamps and amphorae, fluted *kernoi* had been prepared for the great festival of Demeter. The fighting was even carried into the temples: bullets lie amidst the offerings in the *tophet*. Not far from there, under the present station of Salammbo, Dr. Carton excavated in 1916 a whole chapel where the religious material, statuettes of enthroned goddesses or armoured gods, masks of Medusa, lamps and offerings, were still lying on the sacred bench which surrounded the cella. The atrocious battle ended in the sanct-uary of Eschmoun which overlooked the town, not on the present hill of Saint-Louis but on a more northerly hill whose slopes later supported the tiers of the Roman theatre. Repeating once again the sacrifice of Dido, the wife of Hasdrubal, the despotic leader who had directed the resistance but faltered at the supreme moment and gave himself up to Scipio, threw herself and her two children into the fire lit by the Roman deserters, who expected no mercy from the victors.

VII

THE SURVIVAL OF CARTHAGE

THE treatment of conquered Carthage will always be remembered as
the most terrible example of the total annihilation of a nation. The
city was burnt to ashes, the ruins razed to the very foundations, the
soil was scattered with salt, survivors were sold into slavery, and even
the gods were taken to Rome on the promise of being worshipped
there if they would care to abandon their Carthaginian adherents.
Nevertheless, this relentlessness could not altogether destroy the
civilisation which was its victim. Before the last African stopped
speaking Punic, nearly as much time had passed since the victory of
Scipio as between the victory of Scipio and the landing of Dido.
Even in the palace of the Caesars, some of the relations of the
Emperor—himself a man of the Phœnician race—did not know Latin.
The Roman song-writers joked about "Hannibal's revenge"—a com-
pletely pacific revenge, moreover, which did not prevent Septimius
Severus being one of the most energetic defenders of the Empire and
a Roman patriot strongly attached to the grandeur of the *Urbs*.

The surprising survival of Carthage has many causes and aspects.
The very enemies who fought against it were perhaps its best agents.
There was in the first place Rome, whose entirely political hatred had
been directed at the annihilation of a state and not of a culture. Like
almost all the ancient peoples, the Latins, happily for them, knew
nothing of racialism. They had destroyed Carthage because they feared
its recovery and not at all in order to preserve humanity from evil
ideas. They inflicted the same fate on the other Phœnician towns in
Africa which had remained loyal to their metropolis. But those which
were guilty of opportunistic betrayal were allowed by Rome to retain
their political and religious institutions and their culture. Seven received the status of free towns, which officially made them allies and
not subjects of Rome. These were mainly the ports, spaced out along
the Tunisian coasts: Utica, which despite its autonomy, held the
residence of the Roman Governor, and Hadrumetum, the capital of
Byzacium—as its heir Susa is still capital of the Sahel—were the two
most important. In the territory which fell to the Numidian kings,
the three emporia of Tripolitania maintained fruitful relations with

[75] Greek shield sculptured on the frieze of the "Kbor Klib", a monumental altar near Zama. The round shield (*aspis*) is placed on two crossed sabres (the handle of one of them can be seen and the chape of the scabbard of the other). The decoration (vitruvian scrolls on the external rim, ovolos and spearheads) is purely classical, as is also the bust of Artemis with the quiver. The image of this goddess was particularly used to decorate Macedonian shields. The architecture and sculpture at Kbor Klib, together with other monuments which have now disappeared at Chemtou, near Bulla Regia, is evidence of the activity of purely Greek workshops in Numidia, at about the beginning of the Christian era.

[76] Remains of the external surrounding wall of Carthage, discovered in 1949 by General R. Duval. The round holes cut in the rock held the bases of the posts which supported the towers and wooden miradors, above the mounds of earth along the ditch.

[77] Bullets, from the siege. Some are marked with letters and signs.

[78] Ivory head of Greek workmanship, found by Ch. Saumagne in the ashes from the fire of Carthage.

[79] Type of African, during the Christian era, in the Roman province. Bust of a worshipper discovered in the sanctuary at Soliman (cf. Ill. 65). Compare the statuette from Carthage in Ill. 70.

[80] Boglio stele. From the area between Mactar and Zama. Can be dated, according to the style of the personages, from the end of the third century A.D. It is one of the last monuments of the African religion, which was then entirely Romanised. Ba'al Hammon has become Saturn. He appears in the paraphernalia of an emperor, escorted by guards in the uniform of the period, with the eagle and victims hovering above. His costume and the *harpe* he holds in his hand come from the Greek Kronos. But the bull upon which he is sitting is reminiscent of the Phoenician god El, whom the Carthaginians called Ba'al Hammon. The essential idea which inspired the monument is borrowed from Phoenician theology: the sacrifice, which creates a supernatural force, determines the divine providence. The liturgy is that of the African mysteries: the dedicant, Cuttinus, is assisted by his wife and children who fill the role of *canistrarii* (basket-carriers) —one of the minor ranks in the hierarchy of the initiated. Thanks to the piety of Cuttinus, the estate is blessed and produces magnificent harvests: notice the swing-plough (still used today by the Tunisians, but they rarely have oxen at their disposal to pull it). Also represented are the use of the sickle, which is also still practised, and the wagons returning with the crops.

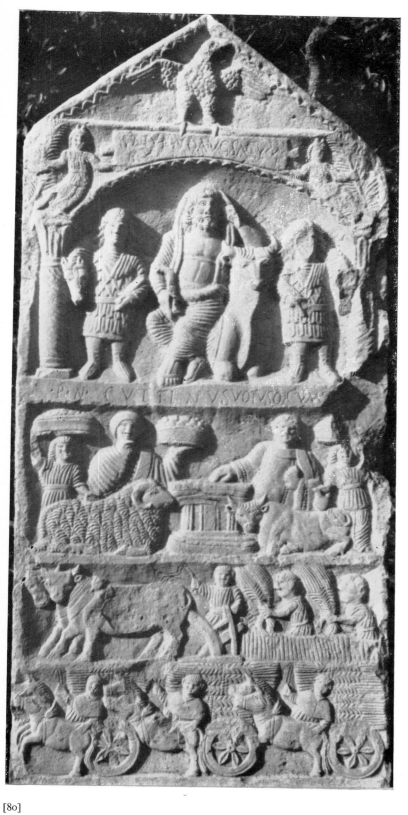

[81] A stele from la Ghorfa. For the general interpretation, see pp. 171-172. The top of the stele, with the symbol of the supreme divinity, is broken. Traces of the symbols for sun and moon, which framed it, are still visible. The anthropomorphous "sign of Tanit" rests on the ridge tile acroterium of the temple. On one side a bird (cock) and on the other a hare, symbolising fertility. In the fronton, bust of goddess with doves.

[82] A stele from la Ghorfa. The supreme god here appears as a bust. Notice the
rendering of the eyes. He holds lightning like Jupiter and reposes on a crescent moon.
The sun is beside him. The two rosettes on either side represent the Star of evening
and that of the morning (Venus). The "sign of Tanit" rests on the enormous crowning
acroterium of the temple. Notice the ornamental treatment of the flowering plants
which appear rising from the acroterium. In the fronton, there is the head of a goddess
between two patera.

[83] Stele from Althiburos. The radiant sun, surrounded by its corona, ending in hands holding palms, overlooks two divinities which can be identified as the *Cereres* by the torch formed by interlocking cups which separates them.

[84] Stele of the same origin, representing the journey of the soul. Above, the soul on a dolphin crosses the upper ocean. The neighbouring symbol (*triskele*) symbolises good fortune. Below, birds facing one another on either side of the tree of life (an old oriental theme) indicate the atmosphere. The two horsemen very crudely represented are the Dioscuri, who represent the two celestial hemispheres. Below, two birds on either side of a fir cone—symbol of fertility and rebirth.

[85] Funeral chambers cut in the rock in central Tunisia. These tombs, which the Arabs call *haouanet*, are often found in central and northern Tunisia, notably in the cliffs of the north coast. Some of them are decorated with paintings (*Photo Combès*).

[86] Mausoleum of Dougga. View of the two upper stories. Notice the pseudo-Ionic colonnade and the entablature formed only of an architrave and a cornice in Egyptian grooves. At the corners of the upper floor, statues of the Sirens can be seen (in antiquity these were always bird-women, never fish-women).

[87] Mausoleum at Dougga. Sculptures on the third storey: chariots and statues of horsemen.

[88] Libyan school at Mactar: horned and bearded divine head. Notice the protruding eyes, the clearly cut angles.

[89] Statue of a lion, undoubtedly funerary. Two others of the same type have been discovered. Lions were still quite numerous in the forests surrounding Mactar at the end of the last century and the Mactar sculptors often drew inspiration from them (see Ill. 64). It is interesting to compare these works with the Assyrian lions (G. Contenau *Man. d'Arch. Or.* III, p. 1304, fig. 824), the Phoenician (ibid., p. 1473, fig. 894), the Hittite (M. Riemschneider, *Le Monde des Hittites*, cover), and Etruscan and Greco-Sicilian (Agrigentum and Himera: see for instance P. Marconi, *Museo naz. de Palermo*, pl. 28 and 42). It can thus be seen how the Asiatic version of the animal was transmitted, soon to be replaced, even at Mactar, by the classical Roman type. The lions of Mactar are closer to the Greek prototype, those of Carthage are more akin to Asiatic models.

[90] Steles originating from the sanctuary of Bu Kornaïn, in the garden-museum of Carthage. They are evidence of the Romanisation of the cult of Ba'al Hammon, who has become Saturn. The inscriptions are in Latin, the dedicants Roman citizens. Note, however, the survival of the stylised sign of Tanit, on the stele on the far right of the first row.

[91] Garden-museum of Carthage.

the Sudan across the Fezzan of the Garamantes. Hippo Regius, today Bône, took advantage of the agricultural development of Constantine to export corn to Italy and the Orient.

The inhabitants of the territory annexed by Rome did not enjoy such advantageous status. Their persons and possessions belonged entirely to the Roman people by virtue of the conqueror's right. In this case, it was not a purely theoretical principle. The land was carefully surveyed and planned so it could be used to best advantage. Traces of this enormous task, which divided all the soil of north-eastern Tunisia into patches of about 800 yards square, are still quite visible. Also, the question was raised on several occasions whether to distribute this *ager publicus* to the Roman proletariat. Actually the African peasants profited from the egoism of the senatorial aristocracy, who preferred to reserve this source of profit for itself and fought the Gracchi before they could realise the benefits of their agrarian law. It was far better to be the tenant of a large absentee landowner than to be forced to give up one's own fields to a little Italian colonist. However, most natives enjoyed the right of occupation on condition that they paid a tithe from the harvest—an obligation not exceeding those imposed by Carthage itself. From the political point of view these stipendiaries depended entirely on the Governor, whose power over life and death gave him the authority of a military commander in time of seige. But this *propraetor* did not trouble to install an administration and therefore recognised the power of the local authorities, elected by the natives, according to the rules of Punic law. The towns and even rural communities thus organised themselves into small republics, most frequently presided over by suffetes. Rome cared even less for the spiritual life of its subjects. The Governor and his auxiliaries naturally used Latin, but Punic remained the language of almost the entire population. The Phœnician gods retained their worshippers. The Senate did forbid human sacrifice but this instruction remained a dead letter in the remoter sanctuaries. At Hadrumetum sacrifices at the *tophet* continued until the end of the first century A.D., but the ex-votos were poor, the symbols engraved on the steles degenerated and intermingled, while the urns only contained ashes of animals. The sanctuary of El Kenissia is situated near the same town, and still contains a *tophet*, enriched with monumental altars and chapels. Most of the rural sanctuaries of Cape Bon are more or less contemporary. The example at Thinissut was dedicated to Ba'al Hammon and Tanit, represented by a lion's head, like the Egyptian Sokhet, but Demeter was there associated with Phœnician gods. At Soliman and Korba, on the other hand, she takes first place. The number of her sanctuaries and their relative wealth point to the Libyo-Phœnicians' attachment to their ancestral religion. Like other peoples deprived of political independence, they rallied round their gods and priests to preserve the national tradition. An association of worshippers was formed in every temple, and the Roman authorities tolerated this. Admission was permitted after an initiation ceremony, reaching its climax in a solemn sacrifice when the worshipper offered himself to the god, magically identifying himself with the victim. This devotion won him material prosperity in this life and admission after death to a paradise situated at the topmost point of the sky, in the ethereal spheres where the stars revolved.

Some, however, were not satisfied either with these spiritual satisfactions or the contemptuous tolerance of Rome for their laws and customs. These people had the initiative to set out for the Numidian and Moorish kingdoms with the certainty of being well received and easily finding a livelihood. Massinissa had not succeeded in realising his dream of annexing Carthage. He had at least wanted to introduce and develop Phœnician civilisation in the principal towns of his realm. Some of them had belonged to the Punic empire. The descendants of the colonists continued to govern them under royal tutelage, enjoying the same freedom which the Hellenic kings recognised in the Greek cities under their hegemony. Others were new creations. Their bourgeoisie was to a large extent autochthonous, consisting of the landowners of the principal areas in the vicinity. But this "gentry" required technicians, artisans, merchants and even intellectuals such as scribes and professors, advocates and priests. Perhaps Massinissa had a momentary dream of creating a Libyan culture. It is not impossible that the alphabet, undoubtedly derived from the Phœnician, which was used to engrave quite a number of inscriptions in eastern Algeria and western Tunisia and which is still used by the Tuaregs, was invented at his court. In any case, the undertaking was abandoned and Punic was the official and academic language throughout the whole indigenous kingdom from the Fossa Regia to the Atlantic. Massinissa's sons carefully collected the libraries of Carthage. One of their descendants, Hiempsal, took pride in having written several works himself. Punic theology in particular profoundly influenced the Libyans, hitherto attached to the most simple forms of animism. A sanctuary to Ba'al Hammon stood at the gateway to every important town. The best known was situated near the principal royal residence of Cirta, today Constantine. Several steles from this *tophet* are dated with the years of the reign of Massinissa and his sons. The same symbols as at Carthage are engraved above the inscriptions, drafted in correct Phœnician, the sign of Tanit surmounted by the crescent moon and the discus, and framed with *caducei*: the palm, the divine hand.

The sacrifice of the new-born continued unabated. Two texts which J. Février has recently deciphered tell of a household which gave birth to a deaf-mute child and did not hesitate to promise this accursed progeny to the gods if they would grant normal children. Another child was born. The unfortunate invalid, already a few years old, was thereupon consigned to the fire.

Hellenes who were settled in the country, and even Latins, associated themselves without any uneasiness with these practices. Some steles are drafted in Greek or Latin, others in Phœnician transcribed into Greek letters—giving valuable information on the pronunciation of words, which the Carthaginians wrote without vowels. The Numidian kings were particularly interested in agrarian cults which favoured the cultivation of the soil. The *Cereres*, Demeter and Koré, worshipped according to Punic ritual, rivalled Ba'al in popularity. Bacchus and Venus also had a large following. The first protected not only the vine but all springtime vegetation as well. The second procured fertility for men and animals. Her principal sanctuary, founded at Sicca (today le Kef) by Sicilian colonists taken there by Carthage in former times preserved the arrangements and ritual of the famous temple of Eryx, on the western point of the island. It therefore contained sacred slaves who prostituted themselves to visitors. It was even stated that young free girls came there from all over Africa to sacrifice their virginity to the goddess.

Punic theologians, imbued with Greek philosophy, then spread a doctrine which introduced a logical order into polytheism: the universe was ruled by a supreme god, soaring above the stars. This Most-High, identified most often with Ba'al Hammon, exercised his providence on earth and man through the intermediary of subordinate divinities: Venus and Bacchus or Demeter and Koré. These doctrines inspired the curious steles of the Ghorfa, which originated in a sanctuary in central Tunisia and most of which are now preserved in the Museum of le Bardo. These may be considered the last phase in the evolution of the Punic stele. They are limestone obelisks, flat and about six feet high, covered with very rich decoration on the front in a curious style which will be analysed below. The supreme divinity occupies the top of the fronton. In order to give better expression to his transcendence, he was not given a human appearance but was only represented in the abstract, with a round face surrounded by a crown or coiled serpent, the symbol of eternity. Below this was a strange character without legs and with a triangular body, not difficult to recognise as the "sign of Tanit". Here, it expresses the creative and life-giving force emanating from the divinity which will spread throughout the universe. Father Ronzevalle has shown that the sign of Tanit was identical with an Egyptian symbol of life, known by the Carthaginians, the "ankh" or "handled cross". On the steles of the Ghorfa, the sign of Tanit carries two cornucopias with a vine escaping from one side, a pomegranate from the other, one consecrated to Bacchus, the other to Venus. The images of the two gods are shown exactly below this vegetation. This is a very clear expression of the idea of the procession of the power of the chthonian gods, masters of earth and vegetation, from celestial providence. These gods look down from the fronton of the temple. Inside, the dedicant, clad in his most beautiful clothes, offers incense on a perfume-pan. Admission into the holy of holies, accompanied by an offering of incense, was the supreme stage of initiation, which assured the worshipper the benediction of the gods during his life on earth and eternal wellbeing after death. It was preceded by bloody sacrifice in front of the temple. Thus, sacrifice retained the essential value attributed to it by Punic theology since its origin. It was in the strongest sense the "creative act of the sacred", or the supernatural force, which even the gods only personified.

These main principles could be modified in the temples to suit the local god, promoted to the status of privileged incarnation of the ineffable All-Mighty. Thus at Althiburos (south-east of le Kef) the celestial divinity appeared in the form of the sun, surrounded by a garland ending in clasped hands. This strange symbol of the sun's benevolence may possibly derive from Egyptian representations of Aton. Here, the serving gods are the Cereres. Beneath the temple, giants and monsters probably represent the infernal powers tamed by celestial envoys and forced to serve them. These bas-reliefs, which can be seen in large numbers throughout the Massylian country, are not only interesting because they compensate for the loss of the theological treatises which were worked out in the temples. They also prove that Punic thought did not die with Carthage, but continued to develop according to its own standards in the fertile collaboration with Hellenism which had been established in the fourth century. There is a striking resemblance between the African mysteries born of this syncretism and the Greco-Oriental religions of salvation. Latin influence only appeared later, when Africans were admitted as equals in the imperial community.

It was not only in the fields of religion and politics that the Numidian realms prolonged the life of Carthage. The Ba'alim—as the citizens proudly called themselves—of Cirta, Zama or Mactar, dressed in the Oriental style in long muslin robes, finely pleated, gathered by a wide belt and covered with a sort of cloak with sleeves, opening down the front. This costume is already found on a third-century Carthaginian statuette. Their women adorned themselves with large "dog collars" and earrings falling to their shoulders. They sometimes covered their heads with high-pointed bonnets, like those worn by Syrian priests at the same period. A charming stele, now preserved in the open-air museum at Carthage, shows a couple: the man wears a long pleated under-robe, a cloak open down the front, and, finally, a sort of apron held up by braces and a belt, falling in rounded folds over his stomach. The woman, who has tightly waved hair, wears two super-posed gowns, the lower one decorated down the centre with a triple-embroided insertion of cloth as in archaic Greek costumes. The strange and stylish costumes are as different from the austere Greco-Roman draperies as from the rough tunics and animal skins with which the nomadic Libyans continued to be satisfied. They could only be suited to a luxurious and easy life and thus bear witness to the prosperity of the Numidian towns and the existence of a wealthy class.

It would not be paradoxical to say that in that "Saint Martin's summer" Punic civilisation, regenerated by Libyan blood, enjoyed a fertility which till then had been denied it. In the first period, however, corresponding to the last two centuries before the Christian era, Numidian art was only an extension of the Carthaginian. Proof of this can be found in the steles of Cirta, which are exactly dated by their inscriptions and absolutely resemble those found in the upper layers of the *tophet* of Salammbo. But fortunately great Numidian monuments of this period have been preserved. Their equivalents must certainly have existed at Carthage but have disappeared without trace. The most important are the monumental tombs. The importance the Libyans attached to the cult of the dead is already known. Ordinary private individuals were satisfied with chambers cut in the rock or dolmens for their last residence. The king, however, who became a god after his decease, sought, like the Pharaohs, to build himself a funeral monument which would defy the centuries. Two famous monuments in Algeria, the Medracen north of the Aurès, and the tomb of the Christian Woman west of Algiers, must have received the ashes of successive Numidian dynasties. These enormous round towers, crowned with a stepped pyramid, belong to a type of mausoleums of Asiatic origin, which the Carthaginians may have introduced into Africa. In any case, their very rustic architectural decoration is borrowed from the Punic repertory. But the Carthaginians generally preferred more graceful funeral towers, square and ending in a sharp four-sided pyramid. One of these mausoleums is represented on a painting in a hypogeum at the Djebel Mlezza in Cape Bon.

But the only one now intact—as a result of skilful restoration by L. Poinssot—stands at the foot of the hill of Dougga. A bilingual Punic and Libyan inscription, now preserved at the British Museum, tells that it was built for Adeban, the son of Yepmatath, the son of Palu, who indisputably belonged to the Numidian aristocracy. The principal architect, Abarish, son of Abd Ashtart, was a Carthaginian, while his collaborators and some of the workmen bore Numidian names. Although the building certainly dates from the second century B.C., its architecture and decoration are related to fifth and fourth century Greek styles. This shows the attachment to archaism which also characterises Punic sculpture. The sculptured decoration at the top of the tower, above the pseudo-Ionic colonnade and the cornice in Egyptian grooves, is inspired by mystical symbolism, the equivalent to that found in western Anatolia in the fifth century B.C. The theme is the journey of the dead, escorted at first by quadrigae and horsemen, then carried by the bird-women, the Sirens, through the air and over the waves, to the distant land of the blessed. A statue of a seated lion at the summit of the pyramid may symbolise the sun god, protector of this paradise, which theologians now situate in the highest sphere of the universe. The journey of the soul through the atmosphere is found again on Numidian steles of a later period. They show the dead crossing the upper ocean astride birds and dolphins. The Babylonians thought that rain originated from a mass of celestial water situated between the air and the zone of fire where the stars revolved, and this naïve belief still survived with the Phœnicians of Africa.

In Numidian realms, as at Carthage, Greeks competed with native artists; they, for instance, carried out the decoration of the Kbor-Klib. Finally, about the beginning of the Christian era, a third school appeared, autochthonous but emancipated from Punic routine. Its development can be followed at Mactar, a fairly remote mountain centre which attained considerable prosperity after the beginning of the Christian era. It first produced some rather rough and ready attempts, such as the horned and bearded head in Plate 88 which may represent a river. Then works began to appear which were at once both clumsy and delicate, such as the head of a helmeted goddess, and soon came genuine successes such as the powerful, majestic funerary statues of lions shown in Plate 89, which revived an old oriental tradition transmitted from Etruria and Sicily. A curious relief representing the god Mars, and dated from 85 A.D., shows how these craftsmen interpreted a theme of imperial propaganda. But after the beginning of the second century A.D., official commissions passed them by and they only retained a local clientèle for the supply of votive or funeral steles. They then succeeded in expressing Neo-Punic theology in a completely original style. Reacting, under the influence of Greco-Roman anthropomorphism, against the abstraction Punic puritanism had imposed since the fifth century, they also managed to avoid becoming academic. The tomb of a priestess of Ceres discovered in the neighbourhood of Mactar is one of the first successes of this style, which was both symbolic and decorative. Its most interesting productions are the steles at Ghorfa and Althiburos. Cut in flat relief, divine, human or animal figures, vegetables and architecture are sometimes stylised to the point of deformity and sometimes minutely detailed. They are set against a neutral background, without any attention to proportions and spatial relationships. These compositions are certainly related to other products of the "provincial" art of the empire, but undoubtedly rather because of a community of intentions and means than because of reciprocal influence. Similarity of inspiration also explains certain resemblances to works of the European Middle Ages, and particularly Indian and Iranian art. The simplicity of these certainly primitive sculptures was regarded with contempt by nineteenth-century archaeologists. Today, the visitor to African museums, perhaps surprised by their similarity to contemporary works of art, finds them more attractive than the vulgar, unimaginative products of the official workshops.

This time, it was not brutal force which put an end to the last developments of Phœnician civilisation. The conflict, latent since Massinissa, between Roman imperialism and Numidian nationalism, undoubtedly provoked, towards the end of the second century B.C., the famous war of Jugurtha, when the hopes of a great African state finally died. Half a century later, Juba I, taking advantage of the Roman civil wars, imprudently tried to resume the great Carthaginian plan of his ancestors, and lost both the crown and his life to Caesar. The short passage of the great dictator, in 46 B.C., can be considered as the point of departure for the only period of Berber history (together with that which began with the taking of Algiers in 1830) when its destiny was linked to the West. Two decisions by Caesar were enough to impose this orientation. The annexation of Numidia brought into the Empire almost all the African countries which were cultivated and inhabited by settled peoples, as well as the very great majority of towns of Punic civilisation. It deprived the native kingdoms—henceforth reduced to the Tell of western Algeria and northern Morocco—of the economic resources and human material to enable them to regain political status. Mauritania was only a protectorate, entrusted by Augustus, possibly not without some irony, to Juba II, the son of Caesar's adversary, who was married to a companion in captivity, the daughter of Antony and Cleopatra.

The reconstruction of Carthage for the Roman colonists created a centre of Latinity—until then almost absent from the province— and this paved the way for the cultural conquest of the Carthaginians.

But almost a century elapsed before the first effects of Romanisation appeared, although, after the beginning of the second century, the conversion of the Africans to the imperial culture developed with astonishing rapidity. The government never encouraged it by constraint or direct propaganda. Even the emperor, Hadrian, advised the people of Utica to keep their traditional laws instead of exchanging them for the statutes of a Roman colony. But reasons of every sort, economic, political and particularly intellectual, drove the Africans to assimilate themselves to a unified society. What advantage did the municipal magistracy have as compared with the authority and prestige of a Roman knight, official of the emperor, or, most of all, a senator? Africa played an ever-increasing part in the imperial economy because of its corn production, which had helped to feed the Roman people for two-thirds of the year since the time of Nero. The bourgeoisie made large profits from this and, not having much idea what to do with them, invested generously in magnificent buildings, which gave the smallest African village the look of a miniature Rome. Many of their sons went to work in Rome. Study of the inscriptions where these new arrivals recounted their careers shows that, at the end of the second century, fifteen per cent of senators and Roman knights came from Africa.

Above all, Greco-Roman culture enjoyed a prestige induced by snobbery. Rhetoric, which was the essential item in higher education, had its attractions for the Africans, themselves fluent speakers. In the middle of the second century, Carthage was spellbound on hearing the best-known writer of the times, who also prided himself on being an orator and especially a Platonic philosopher, a former student of the University of Athens. And yet this Apuleius was born at Madauros, an obscure village, half Numidian, half Gaetulian, as he himself said with charming modesty. Before such a brilliant man and his imitators

—who were many, in even the smallest of the five hundred towns which dotted the African soil—the laggard who still only spoke Punic blushed for his rusticity. The verve with which Apuleius lashed out at his adversaries had to be heard to be believed: his own stepson, he said, was only a cretin who could not and would not speak Latin. The Punic-speaker was only exposed to criticism, but it was the worst of all: he was ridiculous. Also, if he were rich enough, he would hasten to send his son to the brilliant University of Carthage, where Saint Augustine was a professor. Everyone enjoyed themselves very much there, flirting and kicking up a fine shindy.

To tell the truth, for a long time there had been hardly anyone who was completely ignorant of Latin. The most humble African had daily contact with Italians in the same position. Rome, as already mentioned, knew absolutely nothing of racialism and had never prevented its richest subjects from acquiring slaves on the Italian markets, born and bred in that country, and therefore speaking Latin. The inscriptions show that these servants were more worldly than their masters and quickly obtained their emancipation. They immediately played a great rôle in the social life of the city which had adopted them. On the other hand, Rome had dispersed little groups of its citizens outside the colonies, who lived in a large number of native towns, forming a political community apart. Undoubtedly these intruders were not at first very kindly looked on by the autochthons, who must certainly have had to give up land to them. But soon the best-known members of the African community had also obtained the rights of the Roman city and were therefore on a footing of equality with the immigrants. After a greater or lesser lapse of time, the two groups fused, giving birth to a "Roman colony" which was, in fact, mainly composed of naturalised natives.

These processes nibbled away progressively at Punic groups in the various African cities. Even in the ancient territory of Carthage, the Phœnician civilisation had remained primarily urban. It was therefore limited to the social élite, henceforth most strongly attracted towards Rome. This may explain why the rural Libyans could better resist assimilation than the Punics. However, a lively scientific discussion has arisen in recent years on the date of the final disappearance of Carthaginian civilisation. It surrounds the interpretation of several texts by Saint Augustine, showing that the *lingua punica* was still in use in his time (fifth century A.D.) in the neighbourhood of Hippo (Bône), his episcopal town. C. Courtois maintains that at that period the term *punicus* meant nothing more than African, and that the dialect heard by Saint Augustine was in reality Libyan or Berber.

Numerous scholars have protested against this thesis, because Saint Augustine not only affirmed the existence of the *lingua punica* but also noted its relationship to Hebrew—which is abundantly applicable to Phœnician and not at all to Berber. However, it might very well be that Punic was no longer written at that period. The last inscriptions of any length are not later than the first century A.D. and even epitaphs and short votive dedications disappeared at the end of the second century. In the opinion of the author, the political success of Septimius Severus, who came to the throne in 192 B.C., paradoxically dealt the final blow to the cultural traditions of his race. Actually, Punic scarcely survived as the liturgical language with the worshippers of Ba'al, who formed circles remote from imperial society.

Up to the end of the second century, Romanised elements turned away from the religion of their fathers, considered as rustic and barbarous. This situation changed when several Africans assumed the highest offices of the Empire. Many of them considered that they owed their good fortune to the protection of their national gods and, taking advantage of the popularity which foreign religions then encountered at Rome, claimed a place for Ba'al, Tanit and Melqart in the official pantheon. This was not refused them, but the gods, like the men, had to agree to take on the language and customs of Rome. The old native sanctuaries were abolished to give place to classic temples, steles consigned to caves and the priesthood entrusted to the developed bourgeois who called Ba'al "Saturn" and scarcely distinguished him from Jupiter. Already, moreover, Christianity had turned a considerable part of the population away from the traditional cults. Its success was particularly strong in the centres of Punic tradition, as is witnessed by the names of the first martyrs: the pagans made fun of these saints with their uneuphonic names, such as Namphamo which means "good foot". Even in the fourth century, a schismatic sect, Donatism, appeared under fairly slender religious pretexts, raising a movement of dissidence to the Church and Roman Empire and reclaiming for Punic a place equal if not superior to Latin. But no Christian inscriptions written in Phœnician have so far been found. The language of Carthage was now nothing but a dialect, undoubtedly widely contaminated with Libyan. E. F. Gauthier previously supposed that this survival of Punic, which he stretched as far as the seventh century, had favoured the conquest of the country by the Arabs, the Africans finding in the Semitic civilisation as reformed by Mohammed an affinity with their own traditions. But this attractive thesis is scarcely supported by the facts. No Phœnician influence appears in the North African languages. Thus it seems that the language of Carthage, which had survived almost the entire duration of the Roman Empire, perished at the very moment when the Empire itself tottered. However strange this fact may seem, it has an analogy in Gaul when Celtic, still used in the third century, disappeared before the Germanic invasions.

When Carthage died, therefore, it left no spiritual posterity behind it. It did not even, like Egypt and Babylon, leave an artistic treasure which the pick-axe could bring forth one day, to make the thought and sentiments of the dead live again in the minds of future peoples. It is only over the past century that a veritable Punic myth has grown up, born of the attraction exercised by lost civilisations. Carthage for many contemporaries is the lost land, Utopia, engulfed like Atlantis in an inexorable catastrophe. For Flaubert it was a glowing and barbaric society whose refinements and whose cruelties he accentuated. Others became attached to it through sentimental hostility to Roman imperialism. Already in antiquity it was found astounding that fabulous riches whose opulence had rivalled those of Persia could have disappeared without a trace. A Roman knight persuaded Nero that he knew the secret of their hiding-place and paid with his life for the failure of his boast. His present-day successors still sometimes turn to magic or invent strange equipment to track down the lost jewels of the women of Tyre, which are animated— according to one of these treasure-seekers—with a strange life by the initiates who hid them, and are capable of fleeing from the profane archaeologist. Other dreamers have credited Carthage with the same adventures as the famous lost tribes of Israel. They have been taken to America, with the aid of false inscriptions, when the need arose, to testify to their presence. Lacking the real Carthage, the New World has baptised forty towns in the United States with the name of the city of Dido.

This romantic nostalgia leads far away from reality. Nothing is more different than the austere efforts with which historians and archaeologists—Falbe, Beulé, Delattre, Gauckler, Gsell, to name only the deceased—have tried to find the remains of the destroyed city and to clarify them by the evidence of ancient literature. The work is certainly not finished, although the soil of Carthage, covered by the development of the Tunisian centres of population, scarcely leaves any room for scientific exploration. But it is not very probable that new discoveries will greatly change the account we have tried to give. The visitor can appreciate with his own eyes, at le Bardo and at Carthage itself, in the Convent of the White Fathers, founded by Cardinal Lavigerie, or in the new gardens, the museums installed some years ago by the Direction of Antiquities on the site of the *tophet* and around the Thermae of Antoninus. If he feels some disappointment, let him not hastily accuse Rome of having annihilated the work of its rival: enough remains for us to be able to affirm that Carthage, in its desperate eagerness to survive and to draw the most profitable yield from its exertions, never granted to its citizens the free and disinterested activities without which there is no true civilisation.

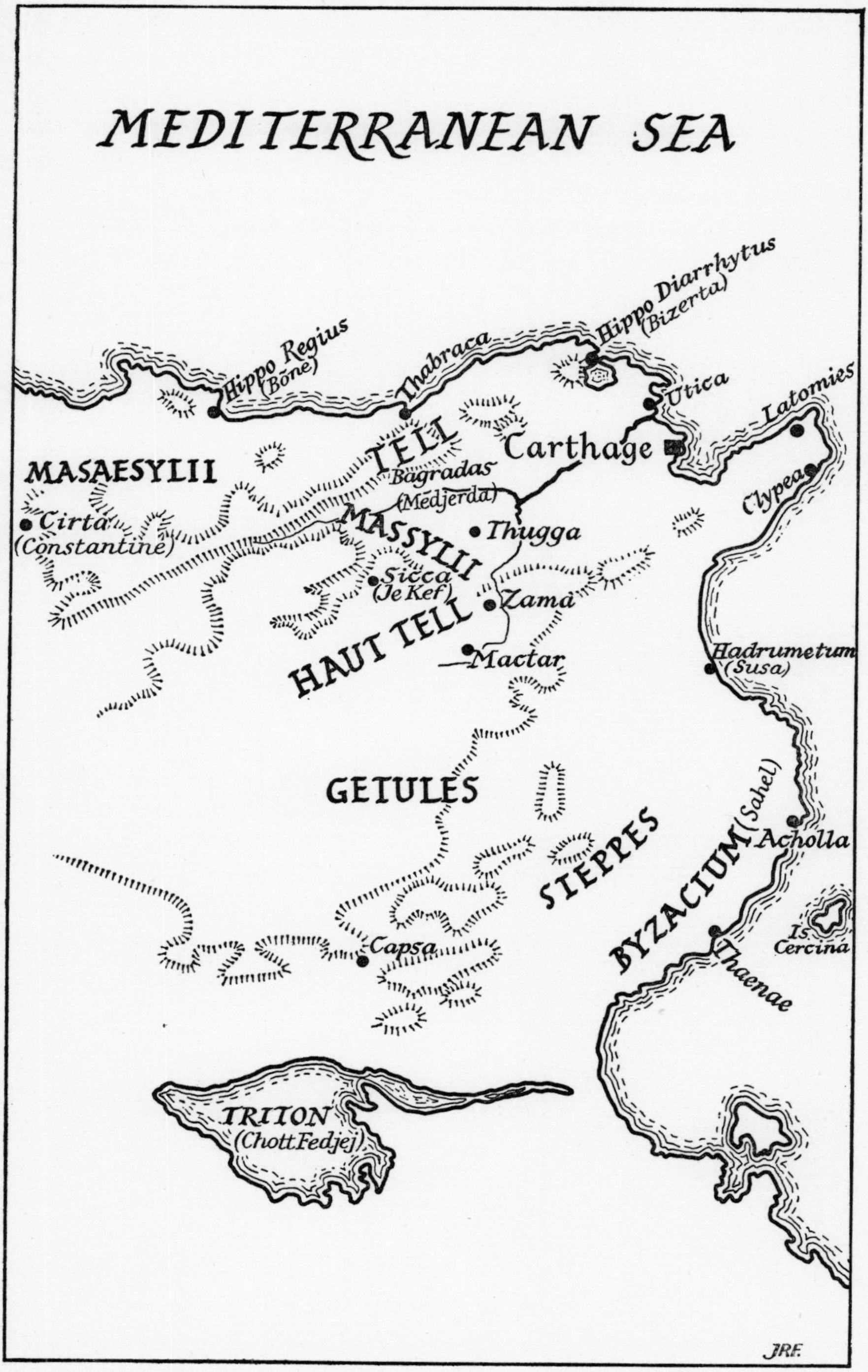

MEDITERRANEAN SEA

Hippo Diarrhytus
(Bizerta)

Hippo Regius
(Bône)

Thabraca

Utica

Latomies

TELL

Carthage

MASAESYLII

Bagradas
(Medjerda)

Clypea

Cirta
(Constantine)

MASSYLII

Thugga

Sicca
(Je Kef)

Zama

HAUT TELL

Mactar

Hadrumetum
(Susa)

GETULES

BYZACIUM (Sahel)

Acholla

STEPPES

Is.
Cercina

Capsa

Thaenae

TRITON
(Chott Fedje)

J.R.F.

APPENDIX

Recent Punic Studies

As a result of the prevailing political situation, hardly any archaeological research has been possible in Tunisia since 1956. Father Féron did, however, continue his excavations on St. Louis Hill, and succeeded in uncovering a large area of dwellings. These researches were described in the *Cahiers de Byrsa*, Vol. 5, 1955, pp. 31–263, and Vol. IX, 1960–61, pp. 77–170, by Father Féron and Monsieur M. Pinard. In their first report these gentlemen attributed the houses they had discovered to the Colonia Junonia founded by C. Caius Gracchus in 120 B.C. In the *Revue Archéologique* 1957, Vol. II, pp. 21–32, I indicated my reasons for believing them to be Punic, dating from the second half of the second century.

As far as other sites are concerned, the one at Kerkouane has been extensively cleared by the Tunisian National Institute of Archæology, but nothing has so far been published. This is a Punic city dating from the third and second centuries, with streets, squares and houses, several of which are Hellenistic in style. One of them (Pl. 50) has a patio with nine columns; others have courtyards. In the centre of one of these courtyards there is a small altar covered with red stucco. Almost all the houses contain a bathroom of the same type as that shown in Pl. 50. Many of the rooms are paved with cement inlaid with marble.

An interesting discovery concerning the town's private life was that of a group depicting bakers, published by P. Cintas in *Oriens Antiquus*, 1, 2, 1962, pp. 232–244.

At Hadrumetum (Susa), L. Foucher has discovered some Punic tombs under the *casbah*. These are as yet unpublished.

On the Punic bronze industry, see C. Picard, *Les oenochoés de bronze de Carthage*, Rev. Arch. I, 1959, pp. 29–64.

M. Astruc has made a study of Carthaginian funeral traditions, published in the *Cahiers de Byrsa*, Vol. VI, 1957, pp. 29–58. See also: *Terra Cotta Casts and Reliefs from Ibiza*, in the *Archivo Español de Arqueologia*, XXX, 1957, and *Carthaginian Casts and Reliefs in Terra Cotta*, MEFR, LXXI, 1959, pp. 107–134.

G. Pesce has made a comprehensive collection of our knowledge about Punic Sardinia in *Sardegna Punica*, Cagliari 1960. There are several Punic temples on this island (including the Temple of Bes at Bithia, the Temple of the Via Malta at Cagliari, with an adjoining theatre; and above all the great Temple of Tharros, the most important Phœnician sanctuary in the west); several tophets; many houses and a large number of religious monuments, the most interesting of which carries a representation of naked women dancing round a bætulus.

In Algeria, the most important discovery has been that at Tipasa of the tomb of a Punic sacrifice official, who died at the end of the first century A.D. (J. Baradez, *Libyca*, V, 2, 1957, pp. 221–270). A. Berthier and M. Leglay have published their discoveries of steles at Tiddis (*Libyca*, VI, 1, 1958, pp. 23–58), and it is interesting to compare these with the steles of El Hofra (A. Berthier and R. Charlier, *Le sanctuaire punique d'El Hofra*, 1955).

On Punic Morocco, the work by M. Tarradell, *Marruecos Punico*, Tetuan, 1960, is a synthesis on a scale comparable with that by G. Pesce on Sardinia. The author covers the Punic ports on the Northern coast of the Maghreb, the Melilla necropolis, the sites on the Rif coast, Tamuda (where a Hellenistic city with a cadastral plan has been discovered), and Lixus, which he has excavated himself, publishing a separate book about it at Tetuan in 1959. There and at Tamuda several areas of Punic city of the Hellenistic period have been excavated. One chapter of the same book is devoted to Mogador, which has also been studied by A. Jodin, in the *Bulletin archéologique du Maroc*, II, 1957, pp. 9–40. F. Villard has contributed a very important article on Greek ceramics in Morocco to the *Bull. Arch. Marocain*, IV, 1960, pp. 1–26. Ionian ceramics, dateable from 650 to 500 B.C., have been found at Mogador. This city was abandoned at the beginning of the fifth century B.C., then reoccupied for a time during the reign of Juba II, then again in the fourth century A.D. There is a Roman house, containing some mosaics, dating from this period.

The new discoveries have reopened the question of the periplus of Hanno. Q. Germain has treated it from the philological point of view in his article *Qu'est-ce que le périple d'Hannon? Document, amplification littéraire ou faux intégral?*, in *Hesperis* XLIV, 1956, pp. 2062-48. This work seems to me hypercritical, particularly when the author describes the periplus as a copy of Herodotus; in my view the influence of Herodotus is only discernible in one single phrase, which I believe to be an interpolation. In spite of concentrated research, no trace of the Carthaginians has yet been found either on the Sahara coast or on the European coast of the Atlantic.

Several studies have appeared on the subject of epigraphy. These include: J. G. Février, *Semitica* XI, 1961, *Punic and Neo-Punic Texts relating to the Testaments*—Bocchus the Younger and the Sosii; *Cahiers de Byrsa*, VIII, 1958–9, *Remarks on the Great 'Marseilles' Tariff*, pp. 35–43; *Journal Asiatique*, 1960, *Attempt to Reconstruct the Molk Sacrifice*, pp. 167–185; ibid. 1962, *The Substitution Rite in N'gaou Texts*; M. Sznycer, *On the Neo-Punic Inscription "Tripolitanian 27"*, pp. 45–50.

Röllig and Donner, *Die Aramäischen und Cananeischen Inschriften*, Wiesbaden 1962. This is the first volume of a work on the grouping of inscriptions, among which are mentioned those found in Tripolitania and Tunisia. Only the text is given in this volume; a second volume is to follow containing the translations, and a third with the commentary on the texts.

As far as the internal history of Carthage is concerned, there is a major article by L. Maurin entitled *Himilco the Magonid; Crises and Changes in Carthage at the Beginning of the Fourth Century B.C.*, which appeared in *Semitica*, XII, 1962. Monsieur Maurin propounds the theory that the Magonids remained in power until the defeat of Himilco in 396 and that the oligarchy only came into being then. Researches now in progress seem to indicate that the substitution of steles for cippi in the tophet did not occur earlier than the end of the fifth century. It would be better, therefore, to regard the political and religious revolution as dating from then, instead of from the middle of the fifth century as hitherto.

Aristotle's texts on Carthage have been re-examined by R. Weil, *Aristotle and History*, Paris, 1960, in particular pp. 246ff. This work shows that the philosopher's opinion about Carthage developed during the course of his career. First of all the Punics seem to him to be barbarians; then he admits that their constitution is an excellent one and compares it with those of Sparta and Crete; later still Aristotle is told of Hanno the Great's attempt at a *coup d'etat*, and seems to regard Carthage as a moderate democracy rather than an absolute aristocracy.

For the Barcide period, we must turn to E. S. G. Robinson. In his article *Punic Coins of Spain and their bearing on the Roman Republican Series*, from *Essays in Roman Coinage presented to Harold Mattingly*, Oxford, 1956, Robinson identifies in particular the likenesses of Hasdrubal, Hamilcar and Hannibal (cf. Pls. 25–28). From this, it has been possible to recognise Hannibal in a bronze bust found in 1946 at Volubilis, in Morocco (see Pl. 25). Robinson's study also confirms the fact that the Barcide régime in Spain was really a military monarchy on the Hellenistic pattern: Hasdrubal is wearing a crown, while Hamilcar and Hannibal are assimilated to Melqart-Heracles.

In October 1961, a Congress of Hannibalic Studies was held under the aegis of the Accademia Etrusca de Cortone, who are going to publish the proceedings. The main contributions touching on Punic studies were those of V. Tusa, *La questione fenico punica in Sicilia*; G. Pesce, *Scavi punici in Sardegna*; M. Tarradell, *Problemas de arqueologia de la epoca barquida en la Peninsula Iberica*; G. Susini, *I problemi archeologici della campagna annibalica*; N. Degrassi and F. Bertocchi on the Battle of Cannae; I also gave two addresses to the Congress—on Carthage in the time of Hannibal, and the portrait of Hannibal.

17

BIBLIOGRAPHY

THE principal difficulty for the historian of Carthage arises, as already said, from the insufficiency of available sources.

As no general history of Carthage has been handed down to us, or even any partial evidence by the Carthaginians on themselves—except the Periplus of Hanno —we must turn to:

(a) brief and scattered indications on the origin of the city, its internal history and its relations with the "barbarian" peoples. The most important of these texts are those of Justin who in the second century A.D. abridged the work of the Gallo-Roman historian, Trogue Pompeius, the contemporary of Augustus. Notable here is the story of the foundation of Carthage.

(b) accounts of the Carthaginian wars against the Greeks and Rome. The history of the Punic wars formed an important part of the work of Polybius the Achaean, the greatest Greek historian after Thucydides, who participated personally in the third war, in Scipio's headquarters. The best second-hand evidence is given by Livy and Appian.

The data of literary tradition can—very partially—be complemented by:

epigraphy—Punic inscriptions are collected in the *Corpus Inscriptionum Semiticarum*, under the auspices of the Académie des Inscriptions et Belles-Lettres;

and above all by *archaeology*—the archæological exploration of Carthage has been carried on for more than a century, under considerable difficulties which have often made it less methodical than might have been wished, by:

Le Service des Antiquités de Tunisie, created by France in 1886 and directed successively until 1942 by R. La Blanchère, P. Gauckler, A. Merlin and L. Poinssot;

The Curators of the Musée Lavigerie of Saint-Louis of Carthage, Père Delattre (1878–1928) and Père Lapeyre, who has been succeeded by Père Féron.

Some amateurs, amongst whom Dr. Carton and M. Ch. Saumagne must be mentioned.

A complete bibliography of the accounts of excavations cannot be given here and access to them is often difficult. The book by M. Beule, *Fouilles à Carthage*, 1869, is still useful. The works of P. Gauckler have been collected in the posthumous work *Nécropoles de Carthage*. The principal discoveries have been the object of communications to the Académie des Inscriptions, printed in the reports of its sessions (C.R.A.I.); regular reports are printed in the *Bulletin du Comité des Travaux Historiques et Scientifiques* (B.A.C.)

A bibliography of excavations at Carthage as well as an archæological description of the site can be found in C. Picard, *Carthage* (Les Belles-Lettres, Paris 1951). See also P. Cintas, *Céram. Punique* (*infra* § Iv) p. 45 ff.

But above all it is important to refer to publications by the Museums. The two most important are the Museum of Carthage, administered by the Society of White Fathers, and the Musée Alaoui du Bardo. The Punic collections of the first have unfortunately been only partially published in the *Catalogue* by Ph. Berger and the *Supplément* by A. Boulanger. These works can be partly complemented by: Hours

Miédan, *Les représentations figurées sur les stèles de Carthage* (extract from the *Cahiers de Byrsa*, I, 1951). As for the second, a *Catalogue* has appeared (1899) by R. La Blanchère and P. Gauckler and two *Suppléments*: I (1910) by P. Gauckler, L. Poinssot, A. Martin, L. Drappier, L. Hautecoeur, and II (1921) by A. Merlin, and R. Lantier. The first volume of a new series, *Collections puniques*, I, *Architecture et Sculpture*, by Mme C. Picard, appeared in 1954.

II

The most important work on Carthage, founded on an analysis and interpretation of the traditional literature which must be considered definitive, and on all archæological documentation known at the time of writing, is the *Histoire Ancienne de l'Afrique du Nord* by S. Gsell, which appeared from 1913 to 1929 and comprises eight volumes: the first is devoted to the geography of North Africa, prehistory, the foundation of Carthage and its beginnings. The second studies the town, the extension of Punic domination in Africa, the constitution and internal history. The third is devoted to military history. The fourth is a picture of the Punic civilisation. The fifth and sixth study the native kingdoms. The seventh contains the history of the Roman province of Africa and the relations of Rome with the Numidian kings. The eighth describes the Caesarean conquest. The undertaking was intended to extend to imperial Africa, but unfortunately the author died in 1932, before he could complete it.

The knowledge of S. Gsell, the soundness of his judgment, and the elegance of his style, undoubtedly make this work the masterpiece of the French school of history since the beginning of the twentieth century. Gsell, who had had a classical education, had acquired a knowledge of orientalism and prehistory which is rarely at fault. He never participated personally in excavations at Carthage, and at times P. Gauckler has the advantage over him, particularly concerning the influence of Greek civilisation on Carthage. But if *L'Histoire de l'Afrique du Nord* is dated on some points, it is most frequently because of archæological discoveries made after it was written: thus the picture of Punic religion was made before the discovery of the tophet of Salammbo. However, the work is so powerfully marked by the personality of the author that it is difficult to conceive the possibility of a revised edition. In any case it remains the indispensable basis of all scientific research and the greatest caution needs to be exercised before any of the judgments formulated by Gsell can be revised.

III

By its very perfection, the work by Gsell crystallized Punic studies for a generation. The works which appeared during that period were mainly confined to making it more familiar to a wider public. The best is indisputably the *Histoire de l'Afrique du Nord*, by Ch. A. Jullien, 2nd edition, revised and edited by C. Courtois, Paris, Payot, 1951. The soundness of the author's information, his very lively form, which comes from an attention to up-to-dateness—sometimes even a little excessive— make this work an excellent introduction to the study of the Punic civilization. A comprehensive bibliography makes it suitable for use by students as a text book.

To put Carthage in its historic setting, reference should also be made to the second volume of the *Histoire des Civilisations*, published by the Presses Universitaires (Paris 1954). In this work, A. Aymard has confronted Carthage with Rome, making the essential features of its civilisation stand out very precisely.

Other serious works which also depend on Gsell for essentials, have no very great originality but remain useful for the additional information they contain: G. G. Lapeyre and A. Pellegrin, *Carthage punique*, Paris, Payot, 1942, is particularly valuable for its illustrations, which include several hitherto unpublished ones and the inventory of the Punic collections in the principal museums in Africa and Europe. Moreover, it is also convenient because of its presentation and its summary of articles which are difficult of access.

M. Hours Miédan has drawn material from Gsell and from the most recent documentation to produce a compact summary for the collection *"Que sais-je?"* (*Carthage*, Presses Universitaires, 1949). But the extreme condensation of this book has accentuated the "monolithic" character of a civilisation which was infinitely more varied, depending on the period.

IV

For some fifteen years, P. Cintas has made a remarkable effort to revive Punic studies, by the almost exclusive use of archæology. He used strict methods of excavation, borrowed partly from the prehistorians, but specially adapted for research into Punic monuments: the discovery in particularly difficult conditions of the necropolis at Tipasa illustrates the value of his technique. He also made use of physics for the purpose of precise datation.

Finally, he attempted to classify objects such as the common ceramic products which had previously been neglected because of their artistic mediocrity. His results are principally expounded in the following works or reports:

Céramique punique, Tunis, 1950

Amulettes puniques, Tunis, 1946

Contribution à l'étude de l'expansion carthaginoise au Maroc: un sanctuaire pré-carthaginois sur la grève de Salammbo (extract from the *Revue Tunisienne*, 1947)

Fouilles puniques à Tipasa (extract from the *Revue Africaine*, 1948)

Fouilles à Utique (extract from *Karthago*, II, 1951 and V, 1954)

A very personal style which deliberately breaks with the tradition of archæological literature, and certain extravagances of expression, should not detract from the appreciation of the undeniable progress he made. The problems of the origins of Carthage, its expansion towards the west and its relations with Spain have been put in a new light by his researches, which have also contributed to a better knowledge of religious thought, everyday life and the Punic economy. The very special character of Punic history—which belongs more to the realm of proto-history—to some extent justifies his claim for the primary importance of archæology. He undoubtedly shows excessive confidence in a method the value of which remains very largely a question of the personal qualities of those using it, and even of chance. Several of his conclusions and datations could or should be discussed or corrected. He must also be criticised for judging Punic civilisation too favourably and refusing to recognise its undeniable weaknesses. But he does not dispute

the importance of the influences exercised on it and has, on the contrary, contributed
to bringing them to light.

V

It would be unfair and futile to omit the influence that the literature of imagination has exercised on the renewal of Punic studies. When Flaubert wrote *Salammbô*
he did not intend to do the work of a historian or archæologist, although he took a
lot of trouble to brief himself. In trying to confront the bourgeois mediocrity which
exasperated him with a world which was both refined and barbaric, he naturally
produced a false image—which the knowledge acquired at his time could not
correct.

Few novels have been written about Carthage. Those who allow their imagination to roam over the ruins of the city of Dido find themselves reduced to writing
a pseudo-scientific work. They take care to thrust aside literary documentation,
inspired by the enemies of Carthage, and the documentation of monuments reduced
by Roman fury to miserable debris, or badly interpreted by modern archæologists,
who are blinded by an incurable attachment to the intellectual vice of classicism.

VI

(Bibliography of Chapter I)

No general history of Phœnician civilisation that takes account of the latest
discoveries is available. The most recent general account is R. Weill, *Phoenicia and
Western Asia* (*English translation*, London 1940). Also to be consulted is the *Manuel
d'Archéologie Orientale* by G. Contenau, vol. III, p. 1456 ff. (Paris, A. Picard, 1931).
For the excavations at Ugarit, which have revealed further information about
Phœnicia in the second millennium and about the Phœnician religion in general,
see the bibliography in R. Dussaud, *La Religion des Hittites et des Hurrites, des
Phéniciens et des Syriens*, Coll. Mana (Presses Universitaires), I, 2nd part. The
reports of excavations by Cl. Schaeffer have appeared in *Syria*, which also contains
the texts translated and interpreted by Ch. Virolleaud.

On Phœnician colonisation in the west and the discovery of the western basin
of the Mediterranean, the thesis by V. Bérard, *Les Phéniciens et l'Odyssée*, is now
dated, but the work abounds in ingenious ideas and is based on a deep knowledge
of the Mediterranean. J. Bérard, *La Colonisation grecque de l'Italie méridionale et de
la Sicile*, poses the problem of relations between the Aegean world and the western
Mediterranean in the second millennium.

On trade in tin: R. J. Forbes, *Metallurgy in Antiquity*, pp. 238 ff.

On the first Phœnician settlements in Sicily: J. I. S. Whitaker, *Motya*, London,
1921, B. Pace, *Arte e civilta della Sicilia antica*, I.

On Sardinia: G. Patroni, *Nora*, (*Mon. Antichi*, XIV, 1904). E. Pais, *Sardegna
primo del dominio Romano*. An inscription from Sardinia would be the most ancient
Phœnician text in the west.

On Spain: P. Bosch Gimpera, *Revista de Occidente*, 1928, p. 314 ff.

On the installation of the Phœnicians in Africa, see the works of P. Cintas,
supra §IV.

On North African pre-history, the thesis by L. Balout, *Préhistoire de l'Afrique du Nord, essai de chronologie*, (Paris, Arts et Métiers graphiques, 1955) in conclusion presents a history of the primitive humanity of the Maghreb and includes an exhaustive bibliography. See also E. Gobert, *Notions . . . sur la Préhistoire de la Tunisie* (*Actes du IIe Congrès panafricain de Préhistoire*, Algiers, 1955).

On the eastern Libyans, F. Chamoux, *Cyrène sous la monarchie des Battiades*.

VII

(Bibliography of Chapter II)

THE problem of the foundation of Carthage emerges as follows.

(1) A historical tradition the value of which has been established by S. Gsell, *HAAN*, I, p. 74 ff, dates the foundation at 814. It does not seem as if the recent attempt by E. Forrer[1] to re-open the problem is well-founded. Forrer believes there has been confusion between the date of the foundation of African Carthage, which would not be earlier than the beginning of the seventh century, and that of the Cypriot town of Kition, which the Phœnicians also called Qart Hadasht.

(2) No tomb earlier than the last years of the eighth century has been discovered in Carthaginian necropolises. The dating of these tombs rests basically on the Greek and Egyptian objects that they contain. Amongst the first are very rare proto-Corinthian vases that might have been manufactured about 730–720 B.C. Amongst the second, the great majority of the scarabs were manufactured under the *Saite* dynasty (663–525 B.C.); rare, very much older objects may have been preserved as curiosities. These facts have incited several archæologists: A. Ackerström, *Das Geometr. Stil in Italien* pp. 163–4, P. Bosch Gimpera and E. Frezouls, *Bull. Corr. Hell.*, 1955, pp. 153–176 to date the foundation of Carthage at about a century and a half earlier.

(3) The discovery of the proto-Punic chapel of the tophet by Cintas (cf. *supra* §iv) introduces a new element into the dating. But the pottery contained in the hiding-place contained in this construction (see Pl. 9), dated by its discoverer from the end of the second millennium, is connected with the sub-geometric style of the Cyclades and cannot be earlier than 750 B.C. (P. Demargne, *Rev. Arch.* XXXVIII, 1951, pp. 44–52). Thus there is a gap of over sixty years between the oldest object brought by the Phœnicians to Carthage and the traditional date of the arrival of Dido. We have tried to show in our *Religions de l'Afrique antique*, Paris, Plon, 1954, p. 32, that "the Cintas chapel" implies the existence of an older cult which could have been that of Dido.

Another gap exists between the chapel and the period when tombs become more numerous: the Phœnician pottery in the lower layers of the tophet belongs to types which are very rare in the necropolises. The population of Carthage, which was not very numerous in the eighth century, was therefore reinforced by a fresh influx of exiles towards the beginning of the seventh century.

The coexistence of incineration and burial in the oldest tombs presents a problem: A. Merlin, *Tombeaux de la colline de Junon, Bull. Arch. du Comité*, 1918,

[1] *Festschrift Franz Dornseiff*, Leipzig, 1953. Pp. 85–93.

pp. 288 ff. Cf. P. Cintas, *Céramique punique*, p. 365; elements from the various races would have lived together in the city[2].

On the interpretation of the myth of Dido, see our *Rel. de l'Afr. Ant.*, pp. 34 ff. This also contains the bibliography of the problem of human sacrifice at Carthage; finally see J. G. Février, *Molchomor*, in *Rev. de l'Hist. des Rel.*, CXLIII, 1953, pp. 8–18.

VIII

(Bibliography of Chapter III)

For sources, see supra §§ I–IV. Carthaginian objects of the seventh and sixth centuries merit a careful study which has hardly been carried out, except in the case of ceramics in the work by P. Cintas (§IV). On masks see *Amulettes puniques* by the same author.

For statuettes, M. Astruc, *Cahiers de Byrsa*, IV, 1955.

The development of Carthage is measured by the extension of its maritime relations. Apart from raw materials, the Carthaginians at that time sold precious fabrics to the Greeks, which were still praised by the poet Hermippus in the fifth century (S. Gsell, *HAAN*, IV, p. 105). For Greek objects at Carthage, E. Boucher-Colozier, *Céramique archaique d'importation*, *Cahiers de Byrsa*, III, 1953, pp. 11 ff. For Egypt, J. Vercoutter, *Les objets égyptiens et égyptisants du mobilier funéraire carthaginois*, Paris, Geuthner, 1945. For Etruria, E. von Bissing, *Karthago und seine Griechischen und Italischen Beziehungen*, *Etudi Struschi*, VII, 1933 (a fundamental study, but its conclusions are sometimes disputable); E. Benveniste, *La tablette d'ivoire de Carthage* (ibid. p. 245 ff.). E. Boucher-Colozier, *Les Etrusques et Carthage*, *Mél. de l'Ecole Française de Rome*, XLV, 1953.

The Punic civilisation takes root in the Balearics and on the Spanish coasts: A. Garcia y Bellido, *Fenicios y Carthagineses en Occidente*, Madrid, 1942. A. Vives y Escudero, *La Necropoli d'Ibiza*, Madrid, 1917. C. Roman y Calvet, *Ibiza*, L. Siret, *Villaricos y Herrerias*, Madrid 1908. M. Astruc, *La Necropolis de Villaricos*, Madrid, 1931. The relations, already existing in the prehistoric period, between the Algerian coast and Spain, favoured exchanges: P. Cintas, *Découvertes ibero-puniques d'Afrique du Nord*, *Comptes-rendu de l'Ac. des Inscr. et B. Lettres*, 1953, pp. 52–57. M. Astruc, *Supplément aux fouilles de Gouraya Libyca*, II, 1954, pp. 9 ff, studies the diffusion of decorated ostrich eggs. This technique was already practised by the Capsians. The Carthaginians borrowed it, enriched it and diffused its products in Spain and Etruria. The port of Gunuga (today Gouraya) on the Algerian coast, easily linked by sea currents to Spain, was used for exports. First inhabited by natives, it became a Punic colony in the third century.

Also during the sixth century, Carthaginians began to settle important colonies on the African coasts where only simple trading stations had previously existed. The first deposits of the tophet at Hadrumetum go back to this period (P. Cintas, *Le sanctuaire punique de Sousse*, *Rev. Afr.* 1948), as well as the foundation of the colony of Tipasa (P. Cintas, *Fouilles puniques à Tipasa*, supra §IV). From that time

---

[2]M. Mazzarino, *Fra Oriente e Occidente*, pp. 118 ff has recently taken up an idea already formulated by Dr. Berthollon, that the Phœnicians could have been preceded in Tunis by Greek colonists. The arguments advanced do not carry conviction.

onwards, Phœnician sailors frequented the islet of Mogador, undoubtedly without having a fixed settlement there (P. Cintas, *L'expansion carthaginoise*, p. 88). Finally, Lepcis, or Leptis Magna, in Tripolitania appears to have been founded at the end of the sixth century (J. B. Ward Perkins and J. Reynolds, *Inscr. of Roman Tripolitania*, pp. 76–77).

On the Etrusco-Punic alliance, as well as works on the relations of the two peoples, see J. Heurgon, *Capoue préromaine*, pp. 78–80).

IX

(Bibliography of Chapter IV)

The void in the fifth century has intrigued archæologists for a long time. The disappearance of imported objects makes dating of the tombs very difficult at this period, so that it was long believed they had completely escaped excavation. In fact, fifth century tombs are known and their poverty is disconcerting. P. Cintas, *Céramique punique*, p. 517, *Utique* I (*Karthago* II) p. 27, *Utique* II (*Karthago* V) pp. 144–145. As P. Cintas rightly notes in this last work and as we have ourselves remarked (*Rel. Afr. Ant.* p. 61 ff.) the absence of Attic red-figure ceramics is not only noticeable at Carthage itself and in the territories directly dependent on it, but also in the greater part of the western basin of the Mediterranean.

On the contrary, no gap exists in the Attic series of the eastern basin, even at Cyprus and Rhodes (contrary to what the first explorations led one to believe): cf. for Rhodes, G. Iacopi, *Clara Rhodos*, IV, 1931, p. 21; the red-figure vases discovered in the necropolises of Camiros are all in a severe style. For Cyprus, see E. Gjerstad, *The Swedish Cyprus Expedition*, IV, 2, p. 317. *The Athenian trade, which . . . began to conquer the Cyprus market at the end of the Archaic period, becomes absolutely predominant during the classical period.*

For the economic situation of Phœnicia in the fifth century, see the excavations at Al Mina at the mouth of the Orontes and the conclusions drawn from them by M. Rostovtseff, *Soc. and Econ. Hist. of the Hellen. World*, I, pp. 85 ff: the economic predominance of Athens is absolute, as would be expected from historical data.

The isolation of Carthage was obviously determined by the rapid Hellenisation of Phœnicia. The monuments at the tophet of Sousse prove that it welcomed conservative elements who were faithful to national tradition.

Direct relations between Asia and the Far West could have existed at the beginning of the fifth century: the history of Sataspes is evidence of it. They possibly explain, as P. Cintas believes (*Expansion carthaginoise* pp. 96 ff.) the persistence in Spain and Morocco of the red ceramics with brilliant varnish, which disappeared from Carthage. But these ceramics could not have lasted very much longer there nor have had any great economic importance, as they would otherwise have introduced the Attic products with which the oriental market was inundated. The naval and economic decadence of Phœnicia, Cyprus and Rhodes, and the omnipotence of the Athenian navy until the Peloponnesian war are sufficient explanation of the rupture of the last bonds which linked the Phœnicians of the west to their metropolis.

It is moreover impossible to explain the commercial closing up of Carthage independently of the religious and political phenomena which affected the new Tyre at the same time. Cf. our *Relig. Afr. Ant.* pp. 60 ff, R. Bastide, *Annales* (*Économies, Sociétés, Civilisations*), 1955, p. 422.

On the monarchy at Carthage, we adopt some of the conclusions of J. Beloch, *Klio*, VII, 1907, pp. 19 ff. despite the reservations of S. Gsell, *HAAN*, II, p. 191, but we would place the end of the hereditary monarchy in the fifth century and not only at the end of the fourth.

The date of the conquest of the African hinterland has been established by Gsell. Besides *HAAN*, see his dissertation on the *Etendue de la domination carthaginoise en Afrique* (14th Congress of Orientalists, Algiers, 1905).

The great maritime expeditions always arouse lively—perhaps too lively—interest. The most satisfactory interpretation of the Periplus of Hanno, seems to be by J. Carcopino, *Le Maroc Antique* (cf. also P. Cintas, *Expansion punique*, pp. 90 ff.). Objections by G. Marcy can be disregarded (*Journ. Asiat.*, 1943–1945, pp. 1–57) and are no more valuable than his other works. M. Rousseau, *Hannon au Maroc, Rev. Afr.*, XCIII, 1949, pp. 161 ff. and R. Mauny, *Note sur le périple d'Hannon* in *Comptes-rendus de la première conf. intern. des Africanistes de l'ouest*, 1951, II. pp. 509 ff. and *La navigation sur les côtes du Sahara pendant l'Antiquité, Rev. des Et. Anc.*, LVII, 1955, pp. 92 ff. have tried to limit the Periplus to the Moroccan coasts. It is in any case impossible to identify Cerné with Mogador as they propose to do, because this site was already visited by the Carthaginians in the sixth century. But the Periplus shows that Cerné was discovered by Hanno.

On the Periplus of Himilco, R. Berthelot, *Festus Avienus, Ora Maritima*, Paris, 1934. It would be desirable to catalogue the Carthaginian objects discovered in western Europe: cf. J. Dechelette, *Man. d'Arch. préhist.*

X

(Bibliography of Chapter V)

Hellenistic influence at Carthage has been clarified by P. Gauckler, *Nécrop. puniques*, pp. 520–521. S. Gsell (*HAAN*, IV, p. 449) was wrong to challenge the importance of the spiritual revolution which then occurred. Cf. our *Rel. Afr. de l'Afr. Ant.*, pp. 80 ff. But the Hellenisation of Carthage should not be explained only by Sicilian influence. That of Alexandria must have been predominant, at least since the beginning of the third century. On the Alexandrian askos shown on Pl. 51 below, see Ch. Picard, *Rev. Arch.* On Alexandrian influences in the African cult of Demeter see our communication to the Congrès Intern. d'Histoire des Religions de Rome, 1955. Cf. also on the cult of Demeter at Carthage P. Cintas, *Comptes-rendus de l'Ac. des Inscr.* 1949, pp. 115–119.

The importance of Carthaginian relations with Hellenistic Egypt is not sufficiently emphasised in J. Vercoutter, *Objets égyptiens* (supra §VIII). But it is apparent in M. Rostovtseff, *Social and Economic History of the Hell. World*.

The everyday life of Carthage is best known in this period. For the constructions at Byrsa, C. Picard, *Vestiges d'un édifice punique à Carthage, Karthago*, III, 1952, pp. 117 ff. In conclusion, indications on other Punic buildings. Excavations at Byrsa have been undertaken by Father Féron, who has succeeded in clearing a whole district. The ports of Carthage, excavated by H. Beulé, have recently been dredged, bringing to light some new discoveries. Despite the difficulty of reconciling the results of the excavations with indications by ancient authors, the hypercritical thesis of M. Ch. Saumagne, *Historia*, V, 1931, pp. 173–195, must be completely rejected—though this is the only serious study to deserve mention after Gsell's analysis. Research undertaken in 1947 by Père Poidebard and Commandants Tailliez and Cousteau demonstrated that no "external port" existed in the bay of Kram (cf. Ph. Tailliez, *Plongées sans cable*, p. 108). It is also necessary to consider with some reserve the hypothesis formulated by Colonel Baradez, on the examination of aerial photographs (*Comptes-rendus de l'Ac. des Inscr.*, 1955, pp. 1 ff.).

Cape Bon seems to have been particularly prosperous at that time. Rich necropolises have been excavated there, sometimes, unfortunately, in unfavourable circumstances. E. G. Gobert and P. Cintas, *Les tombes puniques du Jbel Mlezza*, *Rev. Tunis.*, 1939, and *Smirat, Rev. Tunis.*, 1941 describe those excavations which have been scientifically controlled. A curious rural Libyco-Punic society, strongly influenced by Hellenistic civilisation, appears there. Excavation of the village of Kerkouane, begun in 1953 (*Comptes-rendus de l'Ac. des Inscr.*, 1953, p. 322) was unfortunately interrupted by political events.

The Punic "individual" is also best known at this period. Here may be quoted the curious designs on ostrich eggs at Gouraya, published by Mlle. Astruc, *Lybica*, II, pl. VI–VIII (pp. 18–20). If the first represents in our opinion a goddess (Tanit) rather than a priestess, the second shows a hunter, in close-fitting tights, wearing a skull-cap and armed with a light leather shield.

On Hellenistic Punic art, see especially C. Picard, *Cat. du Musée Alaoui*, (cited supra §I), pp. 3–5, 9 ff. (architecture) 25 ff. (sculpture). The most remarkable objects in this respect are the terra cottas discovered by Dr. Carton in a sanctuary, the site of which is now covered by the Station of Salammbo (L. Carton, *Sanctuaire punique decouvert à Carthage*, Paris, Geuthener, 1929) and by M. A. Merlin at Santa Monica (*Bull Arch. du Comité*) 919, p. 225: thrones of divinities, decorated notably with victories of Alexandrian type.

On the statue-sarcophagi of Santa Monica, see, apart from S. Gsell, *HAAN*, IV, pp. 206–209, and the article already cited by E. von Bissing, J. Carcopino *Les influences puniques sur les sarcophages de Tarquinia* (*Atti Pont. Accadem. di Archeologia*, 1, 2, 1924, pp. 109 ff), M. Pallottino, *Mon-Antichi*, XXXVI, 1937, col. 433 ff., and the article already cited by E. Boucher-Colozier, *Mél. Ecole Fr. de Rome*, LXV, 1953, pp. 78 ff. The thesis put forward by von Bissing is not tenable. Mme. Boucher believes that the tombs belonged to the Etruscan colony of Carthage, which is no longer probable. The Greek character of the monuments has been very well brought out by early studies and by those of Carcopino. But their origin in our opinion should be looked for in Alexandria, not Sicily.

XI

(Bibliography of Chapter VI)

Treaties between Rome and Carthage have been the object of numerous works, which particularly discuss the date of the oldest, ascribed by Polybius (III, 22) to the first year of the Republic (509 B.C.). See E. Boucher-Colozier, *op. cit.*, which gives an almost complete bibliography; see also J. Beloch, *Roemische Geschichte*, pp. 307 ff., which adopts an intermediate position between the "traditionalist" and the "critical" views, admitting the treaty but making it over a century earlier.

It can be stated with certainty that a first Romano-Punic treaty was concluded before that of 348 B.C. (see the argument by Beloch). But the text transmitted by Polybius supposes that Rome controlled the Latin-Aurunci coast as far as Circei, and that Carthage controlled Sicily. At the end of the sixth century and in the first years of the fifth, the Romano-Etruscan monarchy probably dominated the whole of Latium (tradition attributes the conquest of Pometia and the dispatch of a Latin colony at Circei to Tarquinius Superbus); the fact that Aristodemus of Cumæ was able to reach Aricia implies that the Volsci had not yet interposed themselves between Latium and Campania. The Volscian drive took place at the beginning of the fifth century, and Rome did not reconquer the Auruncian coast again until a little before the middle of the fourth century (creation of the Pomptine tribe 358 B.C.). As for Carthage, its position in Sicily was never stronger than in the years preceding the battle of Himera. The treaty could not in any case have been concluded during the period 480–409 B.C., when the relations of Carthage with Italy were non-existent. And it is also not at all likely to place it, as does Beloch, at about 400 B.C., when Volscian power was barely broken, and Rome was very far from thinking of resuming a maritime policy. Mme. Boucher realised that in the sixth century, the Romans were considered by the Carthaginians as being part of the Etruscan Empire and that the maritime clauses provided for the other members of the nation naturally applied to them. In 348 B.C., Rome had just reconquered the approaches of Campania, and Carthage after a long interruption had renewed relations with Etruria: the renewal of the old treaty took place quite naturally, although the mediocrity of the Roman navy rendered the clauses concerning Latin trade in the Punic domain quite useless. These clauses are a supplementary argument in favour of an earlier treaty, because they would probably not have thought of introducing them into the new text if they had not been present in the old.

On the causes of the first Punic war, see J. Spatch, *A study of the causes of Roman wars from 360 to 263 B.C.* On those of the second, J. Carcopino, *Comptes-rendus de l'ac. des Inscr.* 1954. On Ensérune, P. Junnoray, *Ensérune*, Paris, de Boccord 1955. On the policy of Hannibal, E. Groag, *Hannibal als Politiker*, Vienna, 1929. E. J. Bikerman, *An oath of Hannibal, Transact. Amer. Philolog. Assoc.* LXXV, 1944, pp. 87 ff. shows that the text of the treaty between Philip of Macedon and Hannibal (Polybius, VII, 9) is a translation of a Punic document. By the same author *Hannibal's covenant, Am. Journ. Philology*, LXXIII, 1, 1952, pp. 1 ff.: what was at stake was not a real treaty, but an agreement made on his own responsibility by Hannibal and not fully committing the Punic State. On the problem of Zama, L. Deroche, *Les fouilles de Ksar Toual Zammel et la question de Zama*, *Mél. de l'Ec. Franç. de Rome*, 1948, pp. 55–104; as against Deroche we think that Zama Regia can be identified with Jama. On the Kbor Klib our communication on *Les monuments triomphaux romains en Afrique, Comptes-rendus de l'Ac. des Inscr.*, 1948, pp. 421–427 (today the monument is interpreted as a monumental altar, and not as the support of colossal statues).

On the third Punic war, G. Walter, *La destruction de Carthage*, 1947. The external fortifications of the town were discovered by General R. Duval: *L'enceinte de Carthage*, in *Comptes-rendus de l'Ac. des Inscr.*, 1949. We locate the temple of

Eshmoun on the hill of the theatre, and not on the hill of Saint-Louis, especially because of the discovery in that place of a monumental Latin dedication to Aesculapius.

XII

(Bibliography of Chapter VII)

For the survival of Punic cults, we refer to our *Rel. de l'Afrique antique*. For the monuments, cf. particularly the *Catalogue du Musée Alaoui* by C. Picard, and A. Berthier and R. Charlier, *Le sanctuaire punique d'El Hofra*, Paris, *Arts et Mét. Graph.* 1954. On the policy of Rome in respect of the provinces, R. Broughton, *The romanisation of Africa Proconsularis*. The problem of the survival of the Punic language has given rise to a lively discussion, arising from an article by C. Courtois, *Saint Augustin et la survivance du punique*, *Revue Afr.*, 1950, pp. 259–282 and by W. H. C. Frend, *The Donatist Church*, p. 58. W. M. Green, *Augustine's use of Punic*, *Studies pres. to W. Popper*, *Univ. of California Publ. in Semitic Phil.*, XI, pp. 179–190. M. Simon, *Punique ou Berbère*, *Mel. Isidore Levi*, 1953, pp. 613 ff. A. Chouraqui *Les Juifs d'Afrique du Nord*, pp. 13 ff. Ch. Saumagne, *La Survivance du Punique*, *Karthago*, IV, 1953, pp. 169 ff. have all completely rejected the thesis of Frend and Courtois and established, it would seem, the survival of Punic as the language spoken until the fourth century inclusive.